Write

FOR YOUR LIVES

D0300367

Joseph Sesitito received his Master of Science in Social Administration from Case Western Reserve University. He is an expert in cognitive behavioral therapy and Ericksonian approaches to hypnosis and psychotherapy and has written and presented extensively in both of these areas. He has pioneered the utilization of cognitive behavioral therapy to enhance creativity and work with young children, and has developed an integrative therapeutic approach called cognitive hypnosis. He has studied Buddhism for 30 years, and is an advanced meditator and teacher in this area. His primary spiritual mentor is Kyabje Gehlek Rimpoche, who was taught by the same junior and senior mentors who instructed His Holiness the 14th Dalai Lama. Following the publication of *Write for Your Lives,* he envisions conducting workshops and retreats to empower the creative efforts of writers.

To contact the author please visit the website www.josephsestito.com

Write

FOR YOUR LIVES

Inspire your Creative Writing with Buddhist Wisdom

Joseph Sestito

WATKINS PUBLISHING

LONDON

This edition published in the UK 2009 by
Watkins Publishing, Sixth Floor, Castle House,
75–76 Wells Street, London W1T 3QH

1 3 5 7 9 10 8 6 4 2

Designed and typeset by Jerry Goldie

Printed and bound in Great Britain

British Library Cataloguing-in-Publication data available

ISBN: 978-1-906787-22-6

www.watkinspublishing.co.uk

*To my mother, LaVerne Marie –
through her kindness and wisdom, I have been
given the most wonderful life.*

ACKNOWLEDGMENTS

There are so many people who I would like to acknowledge that the job seems overwhelming at first. So, I will put into practice one of my pieces of advice from the book – I will give up the idea "I must do the job perfectly well!" Thus liberated from needing perfection, I would first like to thank Michael Mann from Watkins Publishing for seeing the potential in this book to benefit writers of all kinds, and his recommendations have been invaluable. Next, I would like to thank Shelagh Boyd for her work in editing what was at first a much longer and cumbersome document. So for the smoother and more readable book, I give credit to Shelagh almost entirely. I am very grateful to Barbara Vesey for her thorough-going proofreading of the text. The final person from Watkins I would like to thank is Penny Stopa. She provided me with a lot of advice and encouragement along the way.

I would like to thank my primary spiritual mentor, Gehlek Rimpoche for implanting within me the seeds of Buddhist wisdom, which culminated in this book. Rimpoche continues to be the root of my spiritual development. I would like to thank some of Gehlek Rimpoche's other senior students for guiding me – most significant have been John Moran, Ann Warren, Hartmut Sagola, as well as Susan Kirchner and her husband, Bill.

I thank Robert Thurman not only for his Preface, but also for introducing me to Tibetan Buddhism. He is the brightest and most precious jewel on his own now famous jewel tree of Tibet – although in his humility he would deny this. I also thank Glenn H Mullin for supplying the Foreword. His personal teachings have been of immeasurable benefit. These two individuals are pillars supporting the Dharma in our complex modern world.

Thanks also to my talented publicist, Molly Shaeffer, whose magnificent efforts, I believe, will help this book to reach the many people who can benefit from inspiring their creative writing with enlightenment-oriented wisdom.

Finally, I would like to thank Drs Paul A Sears and Michael D Dwyer for the ongoing encouragement and support of my writing, which began some 20 years ago. May they be supremely blessed for the faith they have always had in my capacity to communicate through the written word. Then there are Drs Albert Ellis, David Burns, and Aaron Beck. They brought to me the insights of cognitive behavioral therapy, through which I began to experience my own liberation as a writer. I am particularly indebted to Albert Ellis for writing the Forewords for my previous two works: *Writer, Unbind Your Mind!* and *Conquer the University: Feel Good About Your A's!* Were it not for his encouragement, I may well have given up on writing before I ever got started!

Thanks so much to all of you!

CONTENTS

FOREWORD

In the *Lankavatara Sutra* the Buddha is quoted as saying:

> *2,500 years after my passing,*
> *My Dharma will go to the land of the*
> *red-faced peoples.*

Most Tibetans today take this prophecy to refer to Europe and North America. The faces of white folk easily flush with red when touched by the wind of passion or excitement.

Another Buddhist prophecy speaks about how the Buddhist tradition will last for 5,000 years, unfolding in ten 500-year periods, each of which has its individual character. The first period would be dominated by wandering ascetics, the next by cloistered monks and nuns, the next by the emergence of the Buddhist Tantras, the next with the destruction of Buddhism in India and its spread through Central and East Asia, and the fifth by the emergence of a plethora of "national Buddhisms" in the various countries of Asia.

Buddhism officially passed the half-way mark of its life cycle in 1956, when it entered its sixth 500-year phase. This is the beginning of the period prophesied in the above quotation from the *Lankavatara Sutra*.

Wherever Buddhism has gone, it has been constituted of two foundational elements: the basic scriptures of the Buddha and the Indian masters; and the indigenous treatises of the Buddhist teachers in the new lands where it has grown. The former category of scripture became known through translations, and the latter were generally written in the native tongues of the writers and teachers of these new lands.

This is also the case with Western Buddhism. We now have several thousand translations of the sutras, Tantras and shastras from India available in English translation, as well as numerous works on Buddhist practice, philosophy and so forth, translated from Tibetan, Chinese, Japanese, Korean and many other languages. And we are beginning to build a considerable body of literature written independently by our own Western teachers.

Western psychology has proved to be a popular launching point for Western teachers, especially in literature. Books of this nature, teaching Buddhist principles in a linguistic environment associated with psychology, have become almost ubiquitous. To name but a few, those by authors/teachers such as Jack Kornfield (*A Path with Heart*), Larry Goldstein (*Breath by Breath*), Dan Goldman (*Emotional Intelligence*) and others have come to represent the mainstream of the Buddhist sentiment.

Joseph Sestito has taken the movement in a fresh direction, and given it an altogether different context, with his new book *Write for Your Lives*. Combining his training in the Western psychological disciplines of cognitive behavioral therapy and behaviorism with his study of the Buddhist traditions, he tackles the problem of the creative writing process as an enlightenment-orientated art, as well as a personal spiritual practice. As a therapist who is also a practicing Buddhist, he looks at conscious patterns and structures of mind from both Western and Buddhist perspectives, and presents a picture of how the creative impulse becomes either constricted or released. In chapters with names like "Cognitive Distortions and Root Delusions", "Ten Irrational, Self-Cherishing Beliefs", and "Sources of Transcendent Wisdom for Living and Writing" he leads the reader through a vision of the workings of the creative spirit in its transference from spirit to brain, hand, pen and finally paper.

The idea of utilizing Dharma principles and practices to enrich creative writing is not, however, Joe's personal creation. Buddhist authors over the centuries have relied upon a plethora of such methods. Joe lists many of these sources.

Perhaps one of the most widespread traditional methods for arousing the creative spirit, at least as practiced in the Tibetan and Mongolian tradition, is the use of special mantras and Tantric meditations. These are usually performed in a closed retreat setting.

The Second Dalai Lama, for example, when a young monk in his 16th year, was preparing to write his first real book. (He had already written numerous essays and poems.) To this end he went to a cave used by his predecessor, shut himself in it for a month, and recited 400,000 wisdom mantras. The year was 1491. As he recited, he visualized that lights went out from his heart, filled the universe and brought back all the wisdom of all enlightenment beings past, present and future. This wisdom came in the nature of sacred nectars and in the form of letters and syllables, as well as wisdom symbols. These melted into his body, like snow falling into a lake, becoming of one nature with his spirit. When he felt he had sufficiently heightened his creative spirit, he proceeded with the job of writing.

In the next few decades he went on to write some of the greatest works of his generation, and indeed his century. He performed similar meditation practices as a preliminary to each of these literary creations. Indeed, it might be said that all future Dalai Lama incarnations owe the ease of their success in life to the widespread popularity achieved by the Second as a result of his inspired writings.

Another popular method for arousing the creative writing instinct that has been used by Buddhist monks over the centuries is that of hand-copying inspirational scriptures which contain particular discourses by the Buddha. A favorite is the *Avatamsaka Sutra*, an extremely mystical (and also lengthy) sutra that covers all aspects of enlightenment vision. Hand-copying the words in beautiful script while contemplating their meanings is said to unleash the powers of mind so that they are able to flow forth in wondrous words of wisdom. The practice has been especially strong in China, Korea and Japan.

Both of these practices – mantra retreat and hand-copying scriptures – begin with the practitioner sitting quietly and watching the breath rise and fall until a state of inner silence is established. One then generates the bodhisattva motivation: "I engage in this undertaking (mantra practice, sutra-copying session, etc.) in order to deepen my enlightenment, so as to be of greater benefit to all living beings." Later, when one feels that one's spirit has been sufficiently sharpened so as to be up to the task of actual composition, one makes prayers that the work to be composed will indeed only be beneficial to others.

Finally, the literary creation is concluded with verses of dedication. For example, the Second Dalai Lama concludes his treatise on the *Six Yogas of Niguma* with the verse:

> Through any goodness that may arise
>
> From my elucidating this supreme Tantric path,
>
> May the spiritual mud of living beings be washed away,
>
> And may they attain the diamond mind free from every veil.

Joe speaks in depth in *Write for Your Lives* on the importance of this traditional practice of establishing basic clarity of motivation, mind and spirit. At one point he comments:

> When we write, we don't write for our lives, but instead largely write trash … By doing this, the reader is accumulating a small amount of negative karma that will negatively affect them in this or their future lives.

The passage reminded me of something a British film-maker friend, Graham Coleman, said to me almost 30 years ago when we were working together on a documentary series entitled *Tibet: A Buddhist Trilogy*. Graham had been a successful stage director, but had given it up for documentary film, and stated to me as his reason, "So much of what passes for theater these days is nothing but the dramatization of delusion. It is hard to be involved and maintain a clear conscience."

Some years ago when I was interviewing the Fourteenth Dalai Lama on the future of his reincarnation lineage, he commented that he might be the last in the line. The tradition, he stated, might have become obsolete. He concluded jokingly, "Anyway, I am not the best Dalai Lama, but also not the worst. So perhaps it is best to be last."

I asked him, "Well, if you don't come back as a Dalai Lama, what will you do? You'll be out of a job."

He laughed and replied, "Maybe I'll come back as a dog, a bridge, or a book. Or perhaps I'll come back incognito, as an ordinary American like you."

This idea in Mahayana Buddhism – that the bodhisattvas can not only control their patterns of rebirth, but even come back in the form of inanimate objects such as books and bridges – is not something invented by the Dalai Lama for the sake of that particular conversation. He was drawing upon a 4th-century work by the Indian Buddhist master Asanga that was inspired by Asanga's visions of Buddha Maitreya. To be exact, the Dalai Lama was drawing from Asanga's *Ornament of Clear Realizations*, or *Abhisamaya-alamkara*, in which Maitreya says to Asanga, "The bodhisattva on this level of spiritual evolution can emanate in countless forms, not only human, but indeed even as a dog, a bridge or a book."

Joseph Sestito's *Write for Your Lives* might just be such a bodhisattva emanation, a bodhisattva soul emanated in the form of a book. It takes the bodhisattva spirit, or *bodhimind*, and places it in the context of a self-help manual for those who wish to write, and indeed might even have great experience and skill in the literary arts, but who find themselves constricted by the infamous ghost of writer's block.

Glenn H Mullin,
Ulaanbaatar, Mongolia,
Feb 2008

Glenn Mullin is the author of some 30 books on Tantric Buddhism and Tibetan culture. His best-known titles include *The Fourteen Dalai Lamas: A Sacred Legacy of Reincarnation; The Six Yogas of Naropa; Death and Dying: The Tibetan Tradition; Life and Teachings of the Second Dalai Lama; The Seventh Dalai Lama: Songs of Spiritual Change; The Female Buddhas; The Flying Mystics of Tibetan Buddhism;* and *Buddha in Paradise.*]

PREFACE

I am honored to write a Preface for this lovely book on writing and aspects of Buddhist "enlightenment science." After reading it, at first I found myself in something of a quandary. I am a writer, and I too often suffer from "writer's block", especially when I have gotten myself into some assignment which I've dared myself to do but actually feel a little intimidated about. Reading in this book about all the little mind tricks our egos play on us to prevent us from writing truth to power, it first felt like opening a Pandora's box for all those mind tricks to come rushing forth. So I first felt "writer's block" about writing a Preface to a book about overcoming writer's block! Well, so this was right away a good opportunity to test of the validity of the wisdom of the author and his mentors and of the usefulness of the methods he shares with us.

The book deploys some of the best methods of modern cognitive therapy to help us reverse the negative thought habits that block us from enjoying life, expressing ourselves creatively, and expanding happiness for others. Joe ingeniously connects these methods with the therapeutic teaching of the Buddha and his successors for over 2,500 years. I love this because I am endlessly insisting that "Buddhism", the "Dharma" and its teaching, is not so much "religion" (that which "saves" by being believed), but is very much more "science" (the pursuit of accurate knowledge of reality), and the therapeutic technologies based on such knowledge. This combination of Beck, Ellis and Burns, and Buddha is irresistible to a writer oriented toward enlightenment, whether blocked or unblocked.

When I sat facing a blank page, I found in my mind all ten of the "cognitive distortions" Joe warns us about: all-or-nothing thinking ("I'll never get it done right, so why bother?"), overgeneralization ("prefaces are useless"), mental filter, discounting of the positive, jumping to conclusions, catastrophizing, should statements, and so on. To counter them I used the five-column method, assessed my situation realistically, voiced my emotional thoughts and rationally evaluated them. I soon saw that positive emotions were released the minute I let go of the various negative habits. Then I began to actually enjoy writing the Preface, and the words began to flow! Why shouldn't I enhance the readers' enjoyment of his wonderful book?

The great thing is that the mental yogas Joe teaches us here are very close to the greatest yogas of living well. The four insights he teaches so poignantly in passing on the wisdom of the Buddha and his successors in India, and especially Tibet, are essential to the art of good living, even if you're not a writer.

First, the realization of the actual nature of reality is prime, and we all have the ability to be more realistic, or even ultimately realistic which means "enlightened", truly wise and vastly compassionate. If you remain stuck in a habitual sense of isolated, rigid self, you will endlessly suffer about all your connections in the world of inevitable relativity. You will fight them instead of embracing them. The insight into true freedom – the voidness of the absolute and the relationality of the real – is the only door of liberation. It alone can open the floodgates of joy and love and happiness. For a writer, this insight into realistic mental and physical freedom is the key to achieving the flow required for inspired creativity and the hard labor of fulfilling vision.

Second and third, cutting off the aching of habitual desires and the burning of habitual angers are the next steps toward bliss, once relationality is fully embraced. I am connected to everything anyway, nothing can possibly get lost, so I don't need to vainly try to own it all. And I will remain connected to everyone, so there is no point in exploding aggressively in a vain effort to get rid of anyone or anything. Better to love it all, and then everyone I touch will be more happy, and, increasing their contentment with themselves, they will gradually stop needing to bother me so much.

Fourth, and this is where I knew Joe had a hold of the key practice of Buddha's wisdom and compassion, he teaches in a down-to-earth way the method of turning the undesirable into the desirable, taking advantage of misfortune, turning hardship into happiness. When you realize that the real meaning of your infinitely relational life is to evolve yourself and all others toward greater and greater bliss, then any misfortune becomes simply a challenge to be used to intensify happiness. When even superficially negative happenings are occasions for growth into bliss, there are no longer any misfortunes. It is useless to bemoan my fate that I have yet another task in front of me, such as "prefacing" a book in a time when I'm very busy and don't need yet another task. Instead, I rejoice in the fact that the assignment got me to read a book that might have been left on my shelf for months, in spite of the interesting subject, and in the book I found new inspiration and many useful practices, and I came to understand the immense practicality of my beloved Buddha Dharma in a new way.

So enjoy this book and honor it by making use of it to inspire your creativity and intensify your living – and don't worry if you're not a writer, life itself is the highest art form and you will express yourself, in whatever way, all the better with the help of Joe and his mentors.

Robert AF Thurman
Jey Tsong Khapa Professor, Columbia University
Author of many books, written
one sentence at a time.

INTRODUCTION

Who This Book Is For

This book is for anyone who wants to do almost any type of writing and who wants to go about this task wisely and compassionately. If – for a variety of reasons – you are not writing, this book will help to stop you from self-damning, condemning, downing, and blaming. The self-defeating beliefs and self-preoccupation, which lead to this lack of compassion for yourself, do nothing to encourage robust creativity in your writing and in your life. In other words, this book will help you replace putting yourself and others down with compassion for yourself and others. You will thus become a more liberated, effective writer, endowed with a greater capacity to be of benefit to your readers. At the same time, you will also become more gentle and kind to yourself. And how could you produce a beneficial, inspired, creative piece of writing without self-kindness being part of your writing process?

This book is your first line of defense against what the Mahayana Buddhist[1] tradition, of which the Dalai Lama is now the best-known representative, calls "self-cherishing", as this and other irrational beliefs adversely affect nearly all writers. Self-cherishing simply means being so preoccupied with yourself that you wind up defeating your own best interest, and usually the best interest of others as well. I imagine somewhere in the world are a gifted few who effortlessly sit down to write with a pen or at a computer and fall into a state of flow from their very first word. I would love to meet them. Yet, time and time again, my experience as a therapist has revealed that the same negative thought patterns in clients – regardless of whether I am treating a budding playwright or a college professor, a fellow therapist working on a book, or a poet – cause them to underperform and be much less creative, inspired, and productive. By recognizing and examining your irrational beliefs about your writing, you will get to the root cause of your struggles and suffering.

What this book will *not* teach is, for example, how to write an elegant sentence or how to define a dangling participle. There are already plenty of titles with this orientation on the market that can show you where to put a comma. Instead, this book *will* get to the roots of your writer's struggles and will examine and determine their possible (and often also probable) causes. It will further help you identify which irrational beliefs may be indeed hindering you in the process of composing beautiful, well-constructed sentences with content that is of optimal benefit to other sensitive beings.

People who write, or want to write, often have a bookshelf full of books on *how* to do just that. They can show you the latest publications on how to generate a book proposal guaranteed to get every publisher or agent who reads it to come clamoring to your door. Yet, even if this happened to you, if you're writing *only* for bolstering your ego, then even this attention would not lead you to boundless happiness. These hopeful writers sit at their computers or in front of blank pages with pens in hand and ready to create, and still, nothing comes – nothing that is, except anxiety, frustration, guilt and self-loathing.

I hope this has never happened to you but, if it has, have you wondered why? It may be because you have not established the conditions for truly liberated writing (to be discussed in more detail later in this book), which are really about bringing benefit to yourself and others. Can writing be a fun, fulfilling, and rewarding process during which compassion for yourself abounds, and where the ultimate aim is greater freedom, happiness, creativity and inspired productivity for your audience? Most assuredly yes! The techniques and ideas presented in this book will be as useful to you as they have been to me in my own writing, and to my clients in theirs.

The most important thing for an enlightenment-oriented[2] writer to have is the motivation to help his readers free themselves from their suffering and limitations, and move toward the state of great bliss, compassion, wisdom, and transcendent generosity that is enlightenment. Prior to receiving instruction in the Dalai Lama's Mahayana tradition, people are asked to have an enlightenment-oriented motivation. The same applies also to your writing. If you are approaching it with the motivation to help others in the highest way possible, then your writing does becomes spiritual practice, and it generates positive karma.[3] Strive to have all of your writing driven by this motivation. In addition to this, I have found that when a self-serving motivation fuels my writing, then the process of writing is of no pleasure at all.

On the other hand, for example, this weekend I worked on a chapter of a manuscript titled *Therapist, Heal Thyself!* I was only thinking about benefiting the reader – the writing flowed and the writing process was bliss. When I read what I had written later in the day, it was superb to the point that I felt it was beyond my own capabilities, as if *I* had not written it. It had been written to help therapists, and that's just the way that it turned out! The more you can write without ego, and to benefit the reader, the more enjoyable your writing will be, the more your readers will savor your sentences and be helped by them. So, keep a close watch on your motivation as you write, keep your mind off yourself and focused on the transcendent generosity of bringing to your readers freedom, happiness, skills, and knowledge that will serve them well in this life and their future lives.

Chapter One

THE ROOTS OF THIS BOOK

I wrote this book after significant writing experience myself, particularly in undergraduate and graduate school. I often struggled with writing during most of this time. However, I uncovered several theories in the course of my studies that made writing considerably easier, and these theories I apply to the process of writing in this book. Additionally, I developed a number of techniques and ideas on my own which have helped me to write more frequently, better quality and more easily. Most importantly, key insights from the Mahayana tradition can be helpful not only in terms of liberating you in your writing life, but in your entire life.

The two main psychological theories I apply to the problem of writing are the ideas and techniques of cognitive behavioral therapy and behaviorism. Drs Albert Ellis and Aaron Beck pioneered cognitive behavioral therapy about 55 years ago, and Dr David Burns is the best contemporary writer, teacher and researcher on the subject. The main objective for cognitive behavioral therapists with their clients is to help them to change the irrational and distorted components of their thinking.

This distorted, irrational thinking is very similar to what the Tibetan Buddhist traditions refer to as ignorance. When ignorance is penetrated and wisdom is obtained, the afflictive emotions cease to exist, and then there is a cessation of suffering. The danger in distorted thinking is that it leads to behavior and emotions that are harmful. The Mahayana Buddhist tradition calls these "afflictive emotions" because they are almost like a disease with which you are afflicted that calls for a cure.

I'm proposing that this cure is an enlightenment-oriented motivation and wisdom, especially when combined with the insights of modern cognitive behavioral therapy. These include, among others, anger, hatred, jealousy, rage, and depression. They rob you of their opposites, which include bliss, supreme happiness, inspired creativity, and zest for living and writing. When Drs Beck, Ellis, and Burns help their clients change their irrational, distorted thinking, then the clients' emotions and behaviors become much less destructive and harmful, and instead become more positive.

A personal example of the above relates to the writing of this chapter, which was not written first, as the order of the chapters in this book would imply, but in fact second to the last! I read through the first draft of my manuscript that was ten chapters long when I realized that the book would be more useful if it included an early chapter explaining the specific roots of the book and what it is about. I also added a final chapter in which the reader is challenged to contribute to changing the world. Still, I procrastinated over writing this chapter for about a week, and felt a lot of frustration during this time because of my self-preoccupied, irrational belief, "This chapter will be boring to write and boring for my readers to read."

This is irrational and self-preoccupied because it contains a cognitive distortion that Dr Burns calls "fortune-telling". It is self-preoccupied because it involves a craving that is one of the eight worldly addictions.[4] I was fortune-telling because I could not know ahead of time what my experience was going to be like in writing the chapter, or what readers' personal experiences were going to be like when reading it. Once I started writing, the process felt quite rewarding, and I hope this chapter will be of benefit to you. When I began to free myself from ignorance by challenging my distorted thinking, behaviorally – by beginning to write! – I began to write with a process-orientation (discussed in Chapter Six) and my afflictive emotions vanished along with any trace of procrastination.

Cognitive behavioral therapy deals mainly with teaching clients to change their distorted, irrational thinking, and thereby eliminating what Dr Ellis calls "the negative behavioral and emotional consequences" of such thinking. In my case, these consequences were procrastination and frustration, which would not have existed had my thoughts been free of distortion and irrationality.

In this book, you will be helped to shape your beliefs about writing and life so as to accept yourself, cherish others, and have unconditional serenity. You will learn that you can gain unconditional serenity when you free yourself from what Buddhist traditions often call the eight worldly addictions. This is true even though, as you will see, one of the eight worldly addictions actually involves wanting to be happy rather than wanting to be unhappy. It is because the worldly concern of wanting to be happy leads to your *craving* happiness. Nonetheless, this craving is by definition self-preoccupied, and it ultimately leads to the opposite of happiness. You will also be helped to experience joy in living and being useful to others, even though you will stop craving these things. They will become mere by-products of the manner in which you will be living together with all beings that collectively inhabit the planet.

The second theory at the root of this book is that of behaviorism, developed by B F Skinner, an experimental psychologist. One of Dr Skinner's concepts involves schedules of reinforcement, and the schedule pertinent to writing is the fixed-interval schedule. Dr Skinner put himself on a fixed-interval schedule of writing for two hours a day during the last two decades of his life and he became extremely prolific during those years. This is the main concept from Dr Skinner that we will be applying to your writing of books and articles. It is going to be suggested that you put yourself on a schedule analogous to Dr Skinner's and write for a maximum of two hours a day, preferably in the same environment and at the same time each day, on as many days of the week as possible. Furthermore, you will want to do this with an enlighten-ment-oriented motivation which will make it become part of your experience of living Dharma or living and writing the key aspects of your own spiritual path during every minute of every day.

Other ideas have influenced the writing of this book, although to a much lesser degree than the Buddhist traditions, cognitive behavioral therapy and behaviorism. For example, the work of Alfred Adler concerning social interest has been an inspiration. Social interest involves altruistically making a contribution to others and to society. The titles of relevant books are included in the Suggested Reading section at the end of *Write for Your Lives*. Reading them will help to deepen your understanding of the main ideas of my book and I recommend that you continue to expand your knowledge base and motivation by delving into my suggested readings as much as you can. *Assignment 1.1* has been included to inspire and guide you in this regard.

I now conclude with a preview of the upcoming chapters. In the next chapter you will learn about ten types of thinking errors that cause inaccurate perception and, as a result, cause harm to yourself and others, in subtle as well as significant ways. In the third chapter you will learn about ten specific beliefs that contain cognitive distortions that may underlie your self-preoccupation, and how to surrender these. In the fourth chapter you will continue to transform your mind and achieve greater freedom through learning how to challenge and surrender your own irrational, self-preoccupying beliefs, and how to replace them with those that are more enlightenment-oriented. Chapter Five is entirely devoted to your achievement of unconditional serenity by freeing yourself from the eight worldly addictions. Chapter Six involves looking at how you can write once you have entirely freed your mind from the eight worldly addictions. You can write in a powerful, inspired manner through writing in the present moment, entirely free of anything that previously could have distracted or disturbed you. In Chapter Seven I discuss how you can use your precious human life to the fullest and with supreme motivation – bodhimind.[5] This is the highest enlightenment-oriented motivation that you can have, and it is your drive to free all beings from whatever hinders them in their spiritual development, and to provide them with all of the tools to achieve enlightenment.

In Chapter Eight, the eight key sources of transcendent wisdom for living and writing are presented and explained in detail. You will learn how to tap into these wisdom sources to create inspired manuscripts, which have the potential to supremely benefit others through the power of the written word.

Chapter Nine will empower and instruct you in how to bring your manuscript to market in as professional and polished a way as possible, while showing you how to persevere through rejections.

In Chapter Ten you're going to get an overview of how your life could be, living your spiritual tradition as well as writing in a prolific manner.

Chapter Eleven is completely devoted to how you can change the world through enlightened words, both spoken and written.

Assignment 1.1:
Getting at the Root

In this first assignment, I'm going to ask you to examine some of the roots of this book more carefully on your own. I've given you the broad strokes, so to speak, but, your assignment is to go ahead and really utilize the Suggested Reading at the end of this book. Some of the titles are probably already familiar, since you are reading this book, but, whichever really strike your interest, go ahead and look them up online. If what you learn there still engages your interest, go ahead and purchase the book and give it a thorough reading. And since what you will have been reading will be one of the key roots of *Write for Your Lives*, reading it concurrently will deepen your understanding.

In Chapter Eight, you're going to learn all about reading supremely inspired texts as a source of transcendent wisdom for living and writing. In the Suggested Reading section, I have included inspired texts from other traditions, which are parallel to the Buddha Dharma tradition in theme. For example, the themes and meditation exercises in Thomas Keating's book, *Open Mind, Open Heart*, from the contemplative Christian tradition are parallel to those in Robert Thurman's book, *Infinite Life*, within the Buddhist tradition. Really marinate your mind, body, and spirit in this material, so that the flavor of your entire life is affected in a dramatic, positive way. Explore as many of these roots as you can, and you will find your knowledge, understanding, and enlightenment growing exponentially! And don't just stick to my list. Beyond this assignment, within your own life, be sure to carry on reading to continuously nourish your unique potential for boundless living!

Chapter Two

COGNITIVE DISTORTIONS AND ROOT DELUSIONS

This chapter outlines the ten cognitive distortions that tend to cause feelings of guilt, depression, anxiety, panic, and other negative emotional states, or what certain Buddhist traditions call "afflictive emotions". Cognitive distortions are similar to what the Tibetan Buddhist tradition calls the "six root delusions". especially the root delusions of "ignorance" and "mistaken views". What is central to all of the cognitive distortions is the absence of wisdom. Wisdom is the opposite of ignorance, and when you have it you understand that everything lacks what Robert Thurman calls "intrinsic substantiality". In other words, nothing exists permanently all by itself, independent of everything.

Cognitive distortions are distortions in your thinking which cause you to engage in harmful behavior and to have harmful emotions, thus generating negative karma, in a vicious cycle. Karma relates basically to the consequences of your actions, and the effect that they have on your own mind – do they have a positive effect, or a negative one? A vicious cycle is created because the negative karma creates more cognitive distortions and strengthens the root delusions, which create still more harmful emotions and behavior.

Fortunately, through cognitive therapy techniques and Tibetan Buddhist insights that are being presented in this and later chapters, this vicious cycle can be broken. You can thus move toward the fulfillment of your true buddha-nature. You can cut through the ignorance and mistaken views, or cognitive distortions. These persist in generating negative karma and suffering, and prevent you from reaching the total bliss and freedom which is enlightenment, and which is your birthright.

I wish to give credit to David Burns MD, for identifying and explaining these distortions in his seminal book, *Feeling Good: The New Mood Therapy*. I also wish to give credit to the psychiatrist Aaron T Beck MD, who originally identified cognitive distortions in his classic book *Cognitive Therapy of Depression*. I recommend that you read these books, as they will deepen your understanding of the material presented in this chapter and Chapters Three and Four.

These distortions – and the six root delusions identified by the Mahayana tradition – are the cause of many negative situations in people's lives: marital dissatisfaction, rage and aggression, depression, anxiety, and other forms of suffering – not to mention lack of productivity for a writer! Cognitive distortions lead to behavior and emotions that defeat both writing and, ultimately, life and liberty. They result in your generation of negative karma. The cognitive distortions are twisted, unclear, irrational, and "primitive" – primitive in the sense that they are types of thinking that do not involve the more sophisticated thought processes usually associated with the cerebral cortex. Their prototypes are short, self-preoccupied sentences that race through your mind like, "I must do well" or "Others must cater to my needs." As Robert Thurman likes to quote from one of his teachers, watch out for the irrational self-statement which says "I am the one."

The ten specific types of cognitive distortions follow, with examples of how they apply to you – a person who aspires to live and write, so you can begin to stop this thinking in its tracks and break the vicious cycle!

The Ten Types of Cognitive Distortions

All-Or-Nothing-Thinking

Using this type of thinking, you will see your work as either all good or all bad or you will think of either writing for eight hours on a given day or not at all. This approach is very unrealistic because your work is seldom all good or all bad, and it is constantly changing. In the first instance, the quality of your work is probably gray and not black or white. This holds true for even the best writers.

Let us consider a great philosopher, such as Jean-Paul Sartre. If you read his book, *Existentialism and Human Emotions*, for instance, you will discover the style and content has both good and bad elements. For instance, there is all-or-nothing thinking in much of the material contained in the book. Sartre proposes, for instance, that you are either heroic or weak, whereas most people's personalities contain both elements. You are also constantly changing. Often your behavior will be average; sometimes it will lean toward being more heroic, and other times you will display weakness. When you see even renowned writers such as Jean-Paul Sartre proposing arguments that are not entirely tenable, it can actually be a relief. *Existentialism and Human Emotions* also has a very dry style, which again can be a relief when you observe it because you can realize that every written sentence you produce does not have to be exhilarating.

You can also remind yourself that you are writing to benefit other sensitive beings and this can completely stop you from focusing on how good your writing is, because you are simply focusing on helping the reader. As you develop wisdom, and realize that everything is empty of true existence and so is constantly changing, it will be easier for you to appreciate how ridiculous it is to see your writing, or any other aspect of your life, in all-or-nothing terms. You will learn specific ways to clear your thinking of these cognitive distortions in Chapters Three and Four.

Overgeneralization

Here you may tell yourself, "I never get a lot accomplished during my scheduled writing sessions," or "Since my proposal was not accepted by the publisher, I'll never get a book published!" The first statement is probably not true because it is unlikely that you *never* get a lot accomplished during your writing sessions. You probably get a lot accomplished some of the time, and something accomplished a lot of the time. The second statement is in error because, although one publisher did not accept the manuscript, this does not mean that it will fail to be accepted by *all* publishers or that an improved version will not be accepted.

Overgeneralizations are not true because they are just that – overgeneralizations! You are simply generalizing beyond what is warranted by the facts that are available to you. Overgeneralization is defeating because it tends to inhibit creative action, including writing, and because it leads to afflictive emotions such as anxiety, anger, and depression. These afflictive emotions will result in negative karma, which will produce still more harmful thoughts, behaviors, and emotions. Why not cut through overgeneralization, and thereby cut through self-preoccupation and the resulting negative karma?

Mental Filter

Mental filter means you obsess over a single negative detail about your writing process or something you have written. You are simply not seeing the reality of your article in its totality because you are obsessing over one negative detail – this is going to lead to afflictive, writing-defeating emotions! You are going to experience a lack of inspiration, simply because of your dwelling on a negative detail. For example, let's say that you focus on the fact that you picked an unsophisticated title for your article, and you ignore the fact that the content of your article could be of great benefit to readers. Although it may have been desirable to choose a more sophisticated title, it hardly justifies the end of your writing that you picked a simple one.

Cognitive distortions and self-preoccupation, in fact, go hand in hand. You "love" yourself so much that you think you have to always pick sophisticated titles so that people will admire you. Then, you might ultimately find yourself discontented, wondering if the title you chose is ever sophisticated enough. This will lead you to have further afflictive emotions, negative karma, and more cognitive distortions!

Did you ever think that your unsophisticated title might attract certain readers that a more complex one would have alienated? Your readers might find your title to be fine, but they could take exception to other aspects of your article.

You also are diverting yourself through this distortion from examining more important concerns, such as how will your article benefit other sensitive beings? How will it help them to move them away from delusions, ignorance and hatred, and toward wisdom, compassion, and enlightenment – the fulfillment of their buddha-nature which is their highest inner potential – the potential for enlightenment?

Discounting the Positive

Here you simply disregard your positive experiences concerning your writing. Suppose, for instance, you experience a lot of joy while writing a manuscript, but the manuscript does not get published right away. Discounting the positive would involve telling yourself that this joy does not matter – the product, your book, and how it is received is all that counts. This is illogical because joy does matter. It is part of your legitimate human experience, related to the production of your manuscript. If, on the other hand, you write the book, and it is published quickly, you could still discount the positive. You might stubbornly insist that anyone could have done the same thing. This self-statement is irrational because you are unique genetically, unique in terms of your personal learning history, and unique in your spiritual evolutionary history.

By disqualifying the positive, you are not going to experience contentment. You can experience true contentment and happiness in the here and now by *recognizing* the positive, not discounting it! For instance, regardless of what you have or have not written, or how good it is, you have attained your precious human life and you are making progress toward enlightenment. What could be of greater significance?

Jumping to Conclusions

Mind-reading and fortune-telling are subsets of jumping to conclusions. If you are a "mind-reader" you may tell yourself, "No one is going to think that what I am writing is any good or very important." This is illogical because you do not know what people are going to think about your writing until you write it, and it is read. It is also self-preoccupying, and negative karma will be born out of it. By telling yourself this, you are also assuming the role of "fortune-teller" because you are forecasting how your work is going to be perceived before it is written. Why not just complete your writing project and then let it be judged by how helpful it is to others? By jumping to conclusions, mind-reading and fortune-telling, you are setting up the conditions in your mind to have afflictive emotions such as anger, depression, anxiety or guilt – any of which can fuel writer's procrastination indefinitely!

If you have the idea, for instance, that people aren't going to like your writing, go ahead and simply disregard this idea and focus on helping your readers instead. That makes a lot more sense than worrying about whether people are going to be impressed by your work or not, which is simply self-preoccupied thinking and won't get you very far except into a creative funk, and quite dissatisfied with your life and your writing.

Don't bother forecasting the future, since you are bound to be wrong anyway. Go ahead with your writing and living, seeking to grow in wisdom, and with the drive to benefit your readers – you can then experience inspiration and exhilaration, as opposed to procrastination and depression!

Jumping to conclusions is a gross distortion that brings about anger and many other afflictive emotions. So put some good effort into eliminating it from your consciousness!

Catastrophizing

The sixth type of cognitive distortion is *catastrophizing* or magnification. If you've had a writing session in which your work does not seem to be high quality, or you produced less than you had wanted, you may conclude, "How terrible!" Then you may feel depressed about your writing, and even about yourself, and you may not pick up your pen and paper again for six months. Your chance of improving either the quality or the quantity of your work comes to a standstill. This leads to even more anxiety about how terrible working on your book has become – a vicious cycle!

Notice how self-preoccupying this would be. Just because something did not happen the way that you wanted it to happen doesn't make it terrible, does it? Self-preoccupation leads to catastrophizing which then reinforces self-preoccupation.

You may work hard on a manuscript for a year and then send your proposal off to a publisher or agent. A few weeks later you get an email from the publisher who writes that they may indeed consider offering you a contract to publish your manuscript after a number of suggested changes are made. But you conclude, "This is awful!" "Why don't they accept it the way it is?" "After all of the work I put into it, it's still not good enough for them!" This is an opportunity you have been working for, but because of your catastrophizing and low frustration tolerance, you sink into a depression and never bother to make the requested changes. This opportunity for this book and possible subsequent publications is gone.

Assuming, of course, that the content of your book would have been of benefit to many people, look at the opportunity that not only you have lost, but that your readers have lost as well. In fact, a powerful incentive to overcome your catastrophizing and to develop a more balanced and enlightenment-driven view is the realization that this distortion can deny many people your wisdom and compassion. Because of interdependence, the ripple effect of your giving up catastrophizing can be far-reaching. Not only do you benefit but everyone else benefits as well. The same applies to all of the other cognitive distortions.

Another scenario is that you work hard for two years on a manuscript, complete it and then send your proposal off to a publisher. You wait for a reply, and wait and wait and wait. Six weeks go by, and you receive nothing. Finally, you muster the courage and decide to call. You get the publisher's assistant on the phone, and after a long time on hold, while they "look for your proposal", she comes back on the line and tells you in a sarcastic voice that you had better get a lot more training in writing before you ever waste her time with your "so-called writing" again! Would this not truly be awful? Depending upon your level of freedom from the eight worldly addictions – particularly the addictions to approval and praise – this comment may or may not cause you to suffer.

Even from an ordinary viewpoint, this would be only one publisher's opinion of your book. Perhaps this person was offended by a position you took. Perhaps she did not appreciate your idiosyncratic style that another publisher would appreciate. Or, perhaps you *do* need more technical or stylistic training. But this is still not "awful", it is simply an opportunity to improve. Criticism is not awful. It can even be an opportunity for positive action.

You can even turn unconstructive criticism to your advantage by recognizing the possibility that this seemingly undesirable situation is actually an opportunity. Seeing it as an opportunity would be turning an obstacle into part of the path to enlightenment. There will be a lot more about turning obstacles into part of the path and recognizing undesirable situations as opportunities in the later chapters.

Emotional Reasoning

The seventh type of cognitive distortion is emotional reasoning. Here a writer assumes that feelings are facts. For example, you may say to yourself, "I don't *feel* that the article that I just finished is very good, so it must not be very good." Remember, the way you feel does not necessarily have any correlation to the quality of your work. In fact, your afflictive emotions can be, and often are, the product of cognitive distortions. In fact, almost all feelings and behaviors that are self-defeating or other-defeating are the product of cognitive distortions or root delusions.

As an undergraduate, I once felt very good about a paper that I had written about the attributes of excellent students. I wrote this as part of an independent study with a professor. I turned the paper in and, during my next meeting with this professor, he ripped it to shreds with seemingly valid criticisms. Interestingly, the previous year, I had presented the same idea to a professor whom I considered to be particularly bright, and he had praised it lavishly. Yet, before submitting that paper, I had not felt so good about it. So much for the way that I felt about something having any relationship to the "fact" of how two intelligent people actually responded to it!

Your *feelings* about the quality of your work, and how it will be received, cannot predict how people will actually react to it. Your *feelings* about how productive you will be in a writing session do not represent facts about how productive you will actually be. You might "think" emotionally and say, "I don't *feel* like writing now, so I might as well skip my scheduled writing for today. I wouldn't be productive anyway." This may well be complete self-deception! And how compassionate are you being toward yourself with this type of thinking, and how wise? Not very! This may also be a good way to procrastinate indefinitely. Some of your most productive writing sessions will come when you sit down and write as scheduled, even when you did not *feel* like writing. You will not know until you, at least temporarily, forget your feelings and sit down and write.

Emotional reasoning can also hinder your Dharma practice, or the spiritual practices within your own tradition, if it is different from the Buddhist tradition. For instance, I recently listened to tape recordings of a three-day retreat given by Sogyal Rinpoche[6] in which he made a similar point about doing daily Dharma practices. He stated that sometimes the hardest thing is getting ourselves to our meditation cushion because of *feeling* that our practice is not going to be productive or enjoyable, even though we consistently find them to be blissful and beneficial, once we actually begin.

Emotional reasoning can play a roll in preventing you from doing almost anything, regardless of how beneficial it could be. For example, I had resisted and felt anxious about giving more of my time and resources at my job. Yet, instances of altruism have consistently been the high points of my life, and maybe they were even the high points for those who received my time and resources. For instance, I recently developed some group-therapy activities for the children at the residential treatment center where I work, which was not part of my job description. I simply developed them to give the children a more rich, lively, and helpful series of activities because I saw the need. Even though this didn't directly benefit me, and even though I initially felt resistance, developing these activities and seeing them put into practice was very fulfilling.

Should Statements

The eighth type of cognitive distortion is called "should statements". This type of distortion can make you miserable about many aspects of your life, especially in regard to your writing. It consists of your stubborn insistence that *things should be different from the way they are.* Dr Albert Ellis wisely asked his clients, "Where is the law of the universe that states that this or that *should* be different from the way it is?" The answer he always gave his clients was:

> Only in your nutty head! Only between your two ears –
> nowhere else! You might like it to be different, and work
> toward this, but there's no rule or law that says it
> automatically should be different just because you
> would prefer this!

In other words, "shoulds" only exist in your mind. They have no external reality outside of your mind.

Ignorance, anger, attachment or any of the six root delusions can result from should statements, and Dr Albert Ellis, the key founder of cognitive behavioral therapy, has shown how this distortion is fundamental to all of the others. You can get rid of most or all of your self-cherishing and suffering by identifying and surrendering your "should" statements, and changing them to rational preferences. So by all means, begin to do this at the earliest time possible, starting now!

I commonly encounter these kinds of "should statements" when working with my clients:

- I should write better than I do.
- I should write more quickly than I do.
- I should be able to produce more work in a single session than I do.
- My manuscript should have been accepted by the publisher.

All of the above statements are illogical because they are absolutes and imperatives that don't exist outside of your mind. Why should you write better, quicker or more than you do? Why should your manuscript have been accepted? No reason, except in your head, between your two ears! All that you can logically say is you would *rather* write better, quicker and in greater volume, and you would *rather* have had your manuscript lavishly accepted. If you give up your "should statements" about writing and change them to "would rather statements" you are likely to be more joyful, less frustrated, more productive, and more other-cherishing. Your work will then be based on your altruistic desire to write for the benefit of all rather than fictional "should statements".

From the point of view of Buddha Dharma, "shoulds" are inconsistent with both wisdom and compassion. They are inconsistent with wisdom because "should statements" imply the inherent existence of phenomena. They are inconsistent with compassion because they lead to anger toward yourself if you violate "shoulds" related to your own behavior, and anger toward others when they violate *your* "shoulds" about what *they* should do. The only "shoulds" that are valid are those that are consistent with reality. For example, one should become a published writer when the precise causes and conditions are in place for this to happen. On a supreme level, one should achieve the omniscient state of perfect, complete enlightenment for the sake of all sentient beings when all obstacles have been overcome, all realizations have been achieved, and when all other causes and conditions exist for this state to come into being.

Labeling

The ninth type of cognitive distortion is called "labeling". Here a writer attaches a label to himself or someone else. For instance, you might conclude that you are a "complete loser" because a publisher did not accept your proposal. Not surprisingly, this type of thinking is apt to cause depression! Is it not difficult – or nearly impossible! – for someone who thinks of him- or herself as a complete loser to feel very good? This type of thinking is also likely to further block prolific and inspired writing. Logically, being a complete loser means another publisher couldn't possibly like your proposal, and you could never write another word worthy of publication. Based on this logic, you would be foolish to submit a proposal to another publisher or ever put another thought to paper! What a wasted effort! After all, you're a complete loser!

This thinking is quite distorted and silly when you break it down. But, there is a serious element also. Let's say, for example, that you have some unique and potentially very beneficial insights about what Tibetan Buddhists call *lo-jung* (thought training) or even a very clear way of explaining it, but you don't do so because you believe you are too much of a loser to succeed at this endeavor. First of all, how kind is it to think about yourself in this manner, and experience the depression and other afflictive emotions that will result? It is obviously not very kind at all! Consider the people who would have benefited from your clear explanation of *lo-jung* and the positive effects of this thought training. Also, consider the kindness toward others that will have been withheld. Why not give up this illogical and harmful labeling, accept yourself as a fallible human and thereby move positively in the direction of being kind to yourself, your readers, and ultimately all other sentient beings?

Labeling in this manner is obviously defeating and demoralizing, but more simply, it is also illogical. In the first place, you were never a loser, let alone a "complete" one simply because your manuscript was not accepted. You are a person whose manuscript was turned down by a publisher. Nothing wrong with that! Would you accept a friend who had just had her manuscript rejected by a publisher? Or even 20 publishers? Of course you would and you would also encourage her to keep trying. Then why not accept yourself with that same compassion and encouragement?

Labeling is just as dysfunctional if it is targeted at others. It is equally illogical and self-defeating to conclude that a publisher who did not accept your proposal, is "an ass". This label is writing-defeating because it will generate hostility toward the publisher and make it more difficult for you to work constructively together in the future. Labeling the publisher is also illogical since he may be trying to keep his job and that is as far as he is looking. You are not privy to all the guidelines or circumstances that are in place at the time your manuscript arrives. Perhaps an advance was just given to a writer who submitted a book proposal quite similar to yours, therefore accepting your manuscript would be a conflict of interest. Perhaps the publisher just found out one of his top authors may defect to another publishing house, and revenues on the new book – expected to break into the stores next month – may be affected. Perhaps the publisher had a personal problem that morning, and he simply didn't feel like reading your proposal! He is after all a sentient being just as you are – an unenlightened being who is functioning under the effect of negative karma, root delusions, and cognitive distortions. Therefore, instead of labeling the publisher and making yourself angry at him, it would be better for you to dedicate the positive karma from today's Dharma practice to the release of his suffering! Or if you are coming from a Christian standpoint, you would similarly give up labeling him and making yourself angry and would instead include him in your prayers.

Based upon the rejection of a manuscript, you might also conclude, "All publishers are asses." This conclusion would combine labeling and overgeneralization. To begin with, labeling is a form of overgeneralization. This would be even more detrimental to your writing because it would interfere with a constructive working relationship with *all* future publishers. Taking this labeling one step further, you can see how it might interfere with all your working relationships.

So why not substitute this labeling with self-compassion, compassion for others, and wisdom? Realizing that all phenomena are empty of intrinsic existence will allow you to cut through labeling very easily. This will not only improve your working relationships with everyone with whom you come into contact, it will also enable you to move toward being of benefit to *all* sentient beings, because you will be moving toward enlightenment.

Personalization

The tenth type of cognitive distortion is called "personalization". Here, for example, you would conclude that the rejection of your proposal is based exclusively on the inadequacy of your work, or worse, on your *own* inadequacy. The rejection may have nothing to do with your work being inadequate, and it most definitely has nothing to do with *your* being inadequate. Your essential buddhanature – the potential for enlightenment which is within you and all other human beings – is pure and luminous, hardly inadequate! You have the capacity to transcend samsara[7] and nirvana and achieve just what Shakyamuni Buddha[8] did – the omniscient state of perfect, complete enlightenment for the benefit of all sentient beings. So, how then, could *you* be inadequate?

As an undergraduate I had a professor who wrote an excellent and very comprehensive book about values. It was thought that the book had even more promise than the work of Gordon Allport, whose writings on this subject had become classics. It was, however, rejected by 20 publishers. How could this be? How could a well-written, insightful manuscript be rejected so many times? Perhaps values were not a hot topic at that time, and publishers did not think that there was adequate interest to justify its publication. The manuscript itself was highly commended, and the professor was certainly an adequate person. Perhaps he simply may not have persevered enough in terms of the publication of this manuscript, or his book proposal may not have been powerful enough in terms of highlighting the benefits of the book. I worked with an individual who had her proposal rejected by 199 literary agents, and it was accepted by the 200th, who placed the manuscript at an excellent publishing house and, to my knowledge, the resulting book has been enormously successful and beneficial to readers.

ॐ

Now that you know these distortions and can begin to hear the faulty dialogue in your head, what are you going to do about it? Well, in the next chapter you will learn one powerful method from cognitive behavioral therapy – disputing irrational beliefs – blended with insights from the Tibetan Buddhist tradition, for ripping to shreds ten of your distorted beliefs about your writing and developing more reasonable, enlightenment-oriented beliefs. This combination may be the most *powerful means* for reducing self-cherishing, attachment and craving concerning the eight worldly addictions yet to be developed.

Assignment 2.1
Loosening the Hold of Your Distortions at Home

The next time you are in a creative logjam, in your writing or your life, begin to loosen the hold of cognitive distortions and root delusions on your mind. You may well find your creative waters flowing vigorously in short order when you begin to develop this habit. Let's say you don't know how to handle a difficulty that you are having with your partner – this is your logjam. Your partner works 55 hours a week, whereas you only work a standard 40-hour week, and you've argued about this on a number of occasions, but without much resolution. In fact, since the arguing began, your partner is coming home later and later and is now averaging 60 hours a week at work.

There are many ways that the situation could be approached, but your assignment is to look at it from the perspective of cognitive distortions and root delusions. Anger is one of the six root delusions. So, ask yourself, am I angry at him for being away so much of the time. Most probably, your answer will be a straightforward, "You bet!" Well, notice that your anger is probably encouraging him to stay away longer, not to come home earlier, so you'd better rid yourself of it. Then you will be happier even when he doesn't come home when you'd like, and you'll be more able to be effective at sensibly negotiating without your anger. You can get rid of your anger by looking at your cognitive distortions that are causing it.

Go through the distortions one by one, and ask yourself questions like these:

- As far as all-or-nothing thinking goes, does he always work 55 or 60 hours, or it is sometimes fewer that that?

- Are you overgeneralizing as well? In other words, has this pattern always existed, is he going through a particularly busy time at work, or is this a particularly busy season?

- Do you have this negative detail stuck in your mental filter so that you are dwelling on it and ignoring all of the positive things about your relationship?

- Does "ignorance" play a role? Remember that ignorance is when you see something as being true or existing for all times under all conditions. So, are you looking at your partner's situation of working late hours as having true, inherent existence and never changing?

- Go through each of the cognitive distortions and root delusions and question your own thinking process in this manner.

Remember that phenomena don't exist in this way because they are always changing! The point of this assignment is, anytime that you are in a creative funk in your writing, family life, work life, in school, or anywhere else, to go through each of the ten distortions and each of the six root delusions and ask yourself if it is playing a role. Just the recognition that this brings about will often take you out of your difficulty and into spontaneous creativity. The exercises at the end of Chapter Four involve a systematic way for changing specific dysfunctional, distorted thoughts, but they are more time-consuming. Fortunately, the above will often be all that you need to begin living and writing creatively and productively again.

Chapter Three

TEN IRRATIONAL, SELF-CHERISHING BELIEFS

I n this chapter, ten writing-defeating beliefs are identified and I will show how the cognitive distortions that are inherent in these beliefs may be supplanted with effective writing and other-cherishing philosophies. These new philosophies will encourage you to write and feel good during the process. That is what this book is about – writing sanely, with compassion toward yourself and others. I have combined Ellis' technique of "disputing irrational beliefs" with Burns' method of identifying cognitive distortions and developing rational responses to double-wham each of the self-cherishing, writing-defeating beliefs.

The beliefs are described as self-defeating and irrational from the perspective of cognitive behavioral therapy, but each of them is entirely self-cherishing from a Tibetan Buddhist perspective. Please read on, as this chapter will help you to become more cherishing of others, effective, and unconditionally happy in your writing and your life.

What follows are ten specific irrational, self-cherishing beliefs that I have commonly encountered while working with clients (not to mention working with myself!). Following each belief, the inherent distortions are identified and a more reasonable, other-cherishing response is proposed. You have probably experienced a number of the following ten beliefs.

1. "I'm too young to write."

Cognitive distortions: all-or-nothing thinking, magnification, and "should statements"

Rational and other-cherishing response: "Well, I might be younger than a lot of people when they start writing, but does this make me *too young* to start? It doesn't at all! In fact, the younger I start, the more writing I will do, and the more likely it is that I will optimally develop my writing ability. The more practice I get, the better the likelihood of producing a great, altruistic masterpiece down the road, which could alter the path that humanity is taking.

"Furthermore, if I start writing at my young age, and maintain a beneficent, other-cherishing attitude throughout, the accumulation of positive karma may give me the capacity to produce a great, altruistic work, or to benefit my fellow sentient beings in unforeseen ways. Indeed, as I make spiritual progress, I may see ways of benefiting others that are not clear to me just now. The earlier I start, the more writing workshops I'll attend, the more writers I'll meet, the more writing I'll do, and I'll generally engage in more behaviors that are likely to make me a great writer of books and articles or other enlightenment-producing works in the future. So, nonsense to my idea that I am too young to start writing!

"This idea will not help me, and it surely will not help other sentient beings, because I will not be honing Dharma knowledge and writing skills to ultimately produce works that will help sentient beings to move toward enlightenment. Of course, I am not too young to be reading, learning to do meditation practices, and receiving teachings on the world's great enlightenment-oriented traditions, which will be nurturing the causes and conditions for making me a great writer in the future. I may be young, but I'm never *too* young. Let's get on with writing!"

2. "I'm too old; too much of my life has passed to begin writing now."

Cognitive distortions: all-or-nothing thinking and tunnel vision
Rational and other-cherishing response: "Where is the 'law of the universe' that states that people can't start regular writing after a certain age? Nowhere except in my head! In fact, I may have a good bit to offer as a writer because I am older. Being older, I have many more experiences that can enrich my writing, compared to my younger peers. And since I am older, I'd better get going and begin a regular writing program, as I probably don't have as many years to work with!

"On the other hand, since no one knows when they are going to die, I may live longer than people who are younger than me. I know from Buddha's teachings that sometimes young people die before older people, sometimes healthy people die before sick people, and no one knows the precise circumstances of his or her death. There may even be some latent advantages to my having waited until I am older to begin my writing.

"So, I am going to start writing for one or two hours a day – today! What I need to examine is not so much my age but my *motivation* for starting to write. And if it is based on wisdom, and cherishing others, then it is positive, regardless of how old or young I am. The reverse is true if my motivation is only born out of narcissism and self-cherishing. So again, the key is to not concern myself so much with my age, but to carefully examine my motivation, and generate the most positive, altruistic motivation!"

3. "I have plenty to write about, but I don't have enough time to write a book."

Cognitive distortions: all-or-nothing thinking

Rational and other-cherishing response: "Although I don't have much time to write, I probably could find some time each day to write or even a few times a week. In fact, 'not having enough time to write' can have some hidden advantages in terms of being a productive writer! Since I have a busy life, I am likely to use the 15- or 30-minute time slots very productively. I am likely not to obsess about my writing sessions after they are over because I'll be quickly on to my next activity. The rest of my busy life can be incubation time for the ideas that will come out of my next brief and productive writing session. So, 'not enough time to write' hogwash! I'll use my shortage of writing time to my advantage. Again, what is key is my *motivation*.

"With a positive, enlightenment-oriented drive, how much time I have to dedicate to writing each day, or each week, is not really that important. What I'm doing will have positive karmic consequences, which will come to fruition in this life or future lives. Furthermore, I don't know how much time I will have *in the future* for writing. For example, even though I don't have much time presently, I can put to good, altruistic use the little time I do have. I don't know for a fact that, next year, larger blocks of time won't open up, they could, especially with the positive karma that I'm building through the altruistic drive that propels my writing! If larger blocks of time do open up, I will have gained momentum by making good use of smaller intervals of time now.

"Regardless, I can begin to put my writing talents to use now, knowing that in this life or future lives, I may be able to substantially benefit living beings through the powerful written word. Beyond this, I can do healing and longevity practices, such as Tibetan White Tara meditations, whereby I can substantially increase my life span and health, so that I can benefit sentient beings longer."

4. "I don't have anything to write about."

Cognitive distortions: all-or-nothing thinking and tunnel vision

Rational and other-cherishing response: "My belief here is certainly interesting because it is an intriguing topic to write about! Let's see, the chapter headings could be as follows:

1 The causes of not having anything to say
2 How to overcome not having anything to say
3 The 'incubation' that occurs within the spaces of time between writing sessions
4 How to generate an enlightenment-oriented drive (also known as bodhimind) to have the selfless freedom and transcendent creativity which goes with writing that's for the purpose of helping others, not elevating your ego

"Now do I really have nothing to say? With the above as just some of almost an infinite number of possible examples, I certainly have *something* to say that will be beneficial. In fact, the more that I cut through self-cherishing and ego and focus on being of benefit, I will not only have plenty to write about, but it will flow. [Chapter Eight is devoted entirely to the transcendent sources of your writing ideas, including ten specific sources. In writing that is inspired by these domains with a good motivation, you will benefit others and help to move them toward overcoming obstacles and achieving realizations.] If I want to be the altruistic writer to which I aspire, I'd better get up from in front of the television and onto the seat in front of my typewriter or computer. Then I will begin to articulate what I have to contribute. And, the best way to do this is to write, write, and write some more – while always aiming to benefit the reader in terms of carefully watching their mind, avoiding negativity, and increasing positivity. If I follow this aim, my writing will never get far off track, and in fact, will be spiritual practice fueled by my enlightenment-oriented desire."

5. "What I have to say isn't important, or original."

Cognitive distortions: all-or-nothing thinking, fortune-telling, labeling and overgeneralization

Rational and other-cherishing response: "How do I know if what I have to say is important until I write it, in my unique style, and then present it to my readership? I don't! I can develop an internal recognition of what's important. Any external recognition, such as the need for approval, could confuse the purpose of my writing.

"When receiving Dharma teachings in the Tibetan Buddhist tradition, I am to listen with an open mind as if I have never heard the teaching before. Traditional teachings, such as The Three Principal Aspects of the Path to Enlightenment may be given many times by the same master to the same practitioners·over the course of time. Because it was said before by no means makes it unimportant!

"Similarly, if I write a book or article, maybe I'm presenting something that has been presented many times before, yet maybe my particular touch, particular perspective, and manner of expression will touch readers who have been exposed to the material many times but haven't fully grasped it, or haven't fully taken to heart its liberating essence previously. Only when I prepare and present my writing to my audience will I be able to refine it to be of maximum benefit, and I'd better do this many, many times to act against this irrational belief.

"Even if I wrote many books and articles, and none of them gained any interest at all – which is extremely unlikely if I write a lot – this does not mean that what I have written and my perspective about it is unimportant. *Importance* is only a relative term. What is important to one audience is determined by time, situation and place, and so forth, and could be totally unimportant to another audience. *Of benefit* had best be my watchwords and not *importance* in the sense that it is portrayed in this irrational and self-cherishing belief. Of course, some things are important in a supreme sense – such as the importance of having a Mahayana or enlightenment-oriented motivation underlying my living and writing. My writings, 100 years from now, may be discovered and viewed as highly beneficial. Jesus found little popular acceptance for his teachings in his lifetime, and now he is an inspiration to millions upon millions of Christians. Due to the extremely relative and transient nature of *importance*, I'd better dispense with that label and get on with my writing for altruistic reasons."

6. "I can't express what I have to say."

Cognitive distortions: fortune-telling and all-or-nothing thinking
Rational and other-cherishing response: "Just because I'm not as good as I'd like to be at expressing what I have to say in writing, this doesn't mean that I can't express what I have to say! 'Can't do' and 'Can't do as well as I'd like' are not the same thing! And it would be best for my writing and my life if I don't see them as the same thing, because that could mean not writing at all. And if I don't write at all, how am I going to be able to improve to be as good as I'd like to be?

"So, I'd better break this possible vicious cycle as soon as possible and get on with writing, and improving my writing in the process. And I can do this best when divorced from ego and self-preoccupation, and 'losing myself' instead in the bliss and flow of writing that's based on cherishing others."

7. "I don't have enough training."

Cognitive distortions: all-or-nothing thinking, "should statements" and tunnel vision
Rational and other-cherishing response: "Perhaps I don't have as much formal training as I could, but how does this make it not

enough! I may well want to seek out further technical training to hone my writing skills, but I am not lacking sufficient training now to begin. Any writer could receive *more* training and benefit from it. Writers see the benefit of training, or there wouldn't be writers' conferences. But does that mean they should refrain from writing until they have enough training? This idea could keep my pen still for my entire life!

"Life itself is a constant training ground and will always present new situations that will stretch my writing skills, so I'd better surrender this faulty idea as soon as possible. I can always engage in further training, but I will do this along with my writing projects, and not instead of my writing projects! Furthermore, if I am exercising what Robert Thurman calls the 'generosity transcendence' through my writing – the giving of Dharma in this case – then my writing will have positive karmic consequences. In this life and my future lives, this will improve my writing, as writing itself is spiritual practice and training when it's driven by this transcendent virtue."

8. "Writing my project will be too hard."

Cognitive distortions: magnification, all-or-nothing thinking
Rational and other-cherishing response: "Writing my book may be difficult, but what would make it *too difficult*? Nothing, except my philosophy about writing! In other words, if I am only writing for self-aggrandizement and ego, then it will often seem as though it's too hard. It will be like walking through cement – difficult, hard, toxic, and practically impossible. On the other hand, the opposite is also true! If I realize that 'I' don't exist, except interdependently, and if I have compassion for myself, and if my aim is to benefit the reader, then my writing will selflessly flow. My writing will be spiritual practice – Dharma practice. Pure, holy Dharma. (Or, pure Christian worship, Zen Buddhist meditation, or living and writing the wisdom of the Tao – your writing and living will be the practice

and performance driven by the combustion of whatever transcendent fuel flows into its engine). Since this will have positive karmic consequences, my practice will become part of a positive cycle – the opposite of a vicious cycle. Thus, my writing and capacities to benefit others will become greater in this life and my future lives."

9. "It would take too long to write a book."

Cognitive distortions: magnification, tunnel vision, and disqualifying the positive

Rational and other-cherishing response: "It depends upon whether I believe I have only one life or that a continuation exists – and only partly upon how much time I have within which to work. If I do have the sense that there are future lives, I will approach my writing in a different manner. I will approach it and all other activities in terms of what Robert Thurman calls 'transcendent patience' and the five other perfections. My mind will not become agitated. With patience, I will think deeply on all the points of Dharma teachings, and it won't matter to me how long it takes to write my book, because more time spent will mean more time to contemplate the Dharma about which I am writing.

"I also need to consider my approach. If I assume that I have to write the book all in one session, or in just a couple of sessions, of course the task is going to seem incredibly daunting! And if I'm thinking this way, I'm likely to procrastinate indefinitely, because why would I even start if I see the task in such an unrealistic manner? Instead, I can see myself writing one session at a time, with each session being manageable, and probably even enjoyable. And this is the way I can approach not only my writing life, but the rest of my life as well. Psychologists call this 'successive approximations to the goal', and I'd better stick with this if I want to make progress toward my goals, as opposed to seeing them as menacing, in which case I would just make progress at practicing procrastination!

"It might take a long time to write the book that I want to benefit others – perhaps six months, or up to five years – but, why should this be *too* long? Perhaps if I plant the karmic seeds for prolific, altruistic writing during this life, they will bear fruit in future lives. There is no rule such as too long, except in my head. I'd better dispense with this irrational, self-cherishing myth if I want to accomplish this and other projects.

"Time goes by whether I am writing or not. Let's say it took me ten years to write a book – if I begin writing now, then at the end of ten years I will have accomplished a lot. I will have written a book and, perhaps, even a very beneficial one. Whereas, if I do not begin writing, then ten years from now the time will have still gone by, but I will *not* have written my book. My belief implies that it should take a certain length of time to write a book, and that this amount of time should be short. This is illogical and self-cherishing thinking. I am going to get started writing now, regardless of how long it takes me to complete the final project."

10. "I probably will not get published anyway."
Cognitive distortions: Fortune-telling and disqualifying the positive
Rational and other-cherishing response: "I can remember that from my spiritual standpoint what is most important is my motivation for writing. If my motivation is malevolent, then even if I wrote dozens of books, and they became published best-sellers, I'd just become wealthy in terms of the negative karma that I would accumulate! I accumulate negative karma by any writing that I do with malevolent motivation. I can thus be mindful of my motivation. If it is bodhimind, or the highest enlightenment-driven motivation, then regardless of the book's publication, karmic consequences will be positive. I will be planting the seeds for publication in this and future lives, or planting seeds to benefit sentient beings in other ways.

"Bodhimind is key. Given this motivation, my work may or may not get published, but even if I knew in advance that my work was not going to be published, would this mean there would be no value in writing it? Of course not. There is still bodhimind on which writing is based, the karmic consequences would therefore be positive, and I will make movement toward becoming a Buddha. On an ordinary level, the experience of writing will make the work worthwhile in terms of gaining skill, gaining insights, finding satisfaction in the process of writing, and altruistically occupying my time. Besides, the more I write, the more likely it is that some will be published, simply on the basis of probability. I will improve skills, knowledge and positive karma in my passionate living and writing my spiritual tradition."

ॐ

In the next chapter you will learn four powerful methods from cognitive behavioral therapy blended with insights from the Mahayana tradition, for identifying and surrendering your own irrational, self-cherishing beliefs and replacing them with more logical, other-cherishing beliefs. Again, this combination may be the most *effective means* for reducing self-cherishing, attachment, and craving the eight worldly addictions yet to be developed.

Assignment 3.1:
Use Enlightenment-Driven Self-Statements

Circle five of the ten irrational, unenlightened, writing-defeating beliefs with which you most strongly identify. Then, review the rational, enlightenment-driven responses that have been articulated for these within the running text of the chapter. Go ahead and edit these to make them even more personal, if you'd like. Really individualize the five enlightenment-driven thoughts so that they are best suited to disrupting your own brand of unenlightened, irrational thinking. They will then disrupt the blocks to create a flow in your writing! Once you have done this, then anytime you find that your freedom as a writer is even slightly diminished, spend up to 10 minutes in a meditative state, visualizing yourself in the setting where you usually do your writing, and performing very well, while thoroughly enjoying the process. As you do this visualization, repeat each of your five personally tailored enlightenment-driven thoughts from Worksheet 3.1 (page 42) to yourself.

Worksheet 3.1 has been provided so that you can improvise by inventing your own enlightenment-oriented self-statements, using the rational and other-cherishing responses to the five writing-defeating beliefs you have chosen. Don't necessarily assume that you have to change my responses significantly to make them your own. You may, but on the other hand they may only need minor tweaking for you to feel resonance with them. And don't be a perfectionist about creating your self-statements. Remember, it's better to strive for what works, rather than what works perfectly!

Really say these statements to yourself with emotion, as you do the visualization of yourself writing in a state of flow, as this will enable you to engrain these beliefs in your right brain as well as your left brain. Take advantage of your neuroplasticity, and allow those synaptic connections to be made! You're literally actIvating your enlightenment-oriented neurobiology! Once again, your assignment is to do this any time you feel the least diminishment in the blissful flow of your writing, and even before a writing session to prime yourself for optimal writing, and inoculating yourself from any creative writing blocks.

Worksheet 3.1:
Your Individualized Enlightenment-Driven Self-Statements

1. ....

   ....

   ....

2. ....

   ....

   ....

3. ....

   ....

   ....

4. ....

   ....

   ....

5. ....

   ....

   ....

Chapter Four

REDUCING WRITING-DEFEATING THINKING

A re you ready to start ripping your cognitive distortions and self-preoccupation to shreds? You'd better be, if you want to stop blocking yourself, start living and writing more fully and generating more positive consequences to your efforts. In this chapter you will learn four systematic skills for achieving this. Remember that cognitions are simply thoughts, cognitive distortions are thoughts that contain irrational elements, and modern cognitive behavioral therapy (pioneered in 1955) is a type of psychotherapy which helps people to get rid of the distortions in their thinking so as to free themselves of conditions such as depression or anxiety, replacing them with zest, enthusiasm, and even bliss, combined with productive and creative actions.

Buddha gave a similar teaching, his Dharma, over 2,500 years ago, which is that people can achieve freedom from suffering and attain enlightenment through seeing the true, undistorted nature of reality, which he called "wisdom", and the development of great compassion for other living beings. In this chapter you will see how elements of Buddha Dharma and cognitive behavioral therapy combine to help you liberate or enlighten yourself from blocks to creativity and great happiness in your life and your relationships.

The Five-Column Technique

Dr Aaron Beck developed the first technique at the University of Pennsylvania School of Medicine. Now, the Beck Center for Cognitive Therapy, which is still affiliated with the University of Pennsylvania, trains hundreds of psychologists, psychiatrists and clinical social workers every year in cognitive behavioral therapy techniques. The goal of cognitive behavioral therapy is similar to that of Buddhist traditions at the most fundamental level – the elimination or reduction of negative emotions, along with harmful thought and action. The Five-Column Technique consists of five steps – so far, no surprises!

1. Identify the Writing Situation or Event (WSE)

Your WSE might be that you are nearing the time to begin your scheduled writing session. If you approach this situation and you feel great, energized, and ready to go, wonderful. Forget about this technique for the time being and begin writing. However, let's say you don't feel great. As a matter of fact, you feel a lot of guilt, anger, depression or other negative emotions. These emotions may interfere with your writing or, more likely, they may lead to your not completing your writing session at all. Remember that these negative emotions can be involved with harmful thoughts and feelings and their negative consequences in other areas of your life. This would begin a vicious cycle. If you have any of these negative emotions related to your writing, the Five-Column Technique may be just what the Buddha ordered!

Please refer to the *Figure 4.1* on page 58 for clarity throughout this discussion, and for a blank Five-Column Technique Form, *see Worksheet 4.1* (page 59) – you are welcome to make photocopies of the latter for your ongoing personal use. Begin the worksheet in the first column labeled "Writing Situation or Event (WSE)." In the upper left-hand corner, describe your situation in the most succinct and objective terms possible. Don't write about your self-defeating, negative emotions under this heading. That would just get you off track because, as you shall see, it is your unenlightened thinking that is creating these emotions in the first place, and here you are just writing down the situation that is *triggering* this thinking. Don't write interpretations in this section either – only the facts! For example, under this heading you might write, "I just sat down in my lounge chair with a cup of tea, a pen, and a notebook with plans to do a two-hour writing session." (*See* Figure 4.1 now and throughout this discussion of the Five-Column Technique.) Sometimes after you complete just the first step you will feel better because *as soon as you write it down you will immediately see that there is nothing inherently distressing about it!*

2. Negative Emotions

The next column is called Negative Emotions. Under this heading, list and number all of the self-defeating emotions that you are experiencing. Give each negative emotion an intensity rating between 1% and 99%. For example, your crippling emotions may be as follows: Anxiety, 90%; Guilt, 75%; Anger 50%. Again, sometimes you will begin to feel better after completing this step. After completing step two, ask yourself, "Is there anything about my WSE that leads *rationally* to the feelings I have listed under Negative Emotions?" Most of the time you will answer with a resounding no! You may even laugh out loud because you will see no rational connection between the WSE and the crippling emotions. Let's ask ourselves, do any crippling emotions need to come into existence just because you've sat down with a pen, paper, and tea with intentions to write? Why not experience exhilaration and inspiration instead? Well, that's just what this technique is going to help you do. So, by all means, don't stop reading.

3. Self-Cherishing, Irrational Thoughts

In the third column, Self-Cherishing, Irrational Thoughts, you list and number the self-cherishing, irrational thoughts that you have *about* the WSE. Now we are beginning to identify the unenlightened thinking that is the cause of your crippling emotions. Self-cherishing, irrational thoughts contain cognitive distortions and are irrational because they also involve the deception that you will be unhappy if you do not stay focused on yourself. Actually, forgetting yourself is a lot more likely to bring about spontaneity, creativity, inspiration and enlightened motivation. These thoughts are illogical, lacking in self-compassion, and born out of a self-preoccupied mindset. In other words, they are born out of self-cherishing core beliefs, such as: "I am important, and people must recognize this! They're no good if they don't!" For example, to continue with Figure 4.1, you may have thoughts like:

> "I missed my writing session yesterday, and I shouldn't have!"

> "It's going to be too hard for me to sit here for two hours and write."

> "I'm not going to write anything good anyway."

None of these beliefs logically follows from the WSE. They contain cognitive distortions. To the degree that you believe them, you will make yourself feel miserable and block yourself from the joy of living and writing. This will produce a vicious cycle, psychologically and from the standpoint of karma, so we'd better move on to the medicine contained in step four. That is, the golden elixir of their being transformed into more rational, other-cherishing thoughts.

4. Rational and Other-Cherishing Responses

Step four is where you get to the essence of changing your unenlightened thoughts and transforming them into enlightened ones.

Why *not* do this? You identify the cognitive distortions in your self-cherishing, irrational thoughts that you listed in step 3 above and then change them into enlightenment-oriented responses. These new thoughts will be clear and free of distortions and will reflect concern for other living beings. In other words, they will not be self-cherishing. You start off by making a new heading called Rational and Other-Cherishing Responses to the right of Self-Cherishing, Irrational Thoughts. You look for the cognitive distortion(s) in the first self-cherishing, irrational thought in the previous column.

For instance, what cognitive distortion is in the thought: "I missed my writing session yesterday, which I should not have done. I really should write double today to make up for it." This is a typical example of a "should statement". "Should statements" of this kind are inconsistent with the reality that you didn't write yesterday, and they are lacking in acceptance of this. They are self-cherishing or self-preoccupied in the sense that it is implied that you have an importance that is immeasurable, almost Creator-like.

Such beliefs lack the Buddha's wisdom that you and everyone else are empty of intrinsic existence. You're empty or selfless in the sense that your existence depends on the existence of everything else – you don't exist on your own, independently. "Should statements" assume intrinsic existence and permanence because they lack the flexibility and mutability of the way things actually are. The key insight of the Buddha is that things are selfless, which is to say soft, pliable, free, creative and infinitely capable of change and evolution. So, your enlightened-oriented response to your "should statement" could be something like this: "Where is the law of the universe that states that I *should* have done my writing yesterday? Nowhere is it written when and how much except in my head. It may have been better if I had done a writing session yesterday, but I don't become beyond redemption because I didn't, as my 'should statement' would suggest. Now let's get busy with today's session!"

Let's look at the second self-cherishing, irrational thought listed in the examples in step 4: "It's going to be too hard for me to sit here for these two hours and write." Two cognitive distortions are in this – thought-magnification and fortune-telling. Your second entry under Rational and Other-Cherishing Responses could go something like this: "Before the fact, how do I know that it is going to be *too* hard for me to sit and write for two hours? Even if it does prove to be difficult, how could I prove that it would be *too* hard? I couldn't, because this would be equivalent to my trying to prove that it would be impossible for me to sit down and write for two hours. How illogical! For all I know, I may wind up finding fulfillment in this writing session – unless I try 'too hard' to make it a miserable session. It's possible that I might produce some writing during today's session that will be of enormous benefit. How can I know in advance? All I can do is sit down with an altruistic motivation and do today's writing session. Would I lack the compassion to ask any more than this from someone else – then why ask more than that from myself?"

Finally, what thinking distortions are in the third self-cherishing, irrational thought: "I'm not going to write anything good anyway?" This statement contains two of them – fortune-telling and all-or-nothing thinking. Your third entry would be something like this: "There's no way that I can know – before the fact – whether this is going to be a productive session in which something significant is produced, or not. Even if the session is less productive than I would have liked, the chances are that I would have produced something of value, especially with an altruistic motivation. Rather than making predictions, why not just get moving with an experimental attitude and see how the session turns out? Why not forget about myself, stop being preoccupied, realize my selflessness, and just flow rather than worrying about how well I'm flowing?"

Compare the three self-preoccupied, irrational thoughts with the enlightenment-oriented responses in the last three paragraphs. How do you feel when you use the enlightenment-oriented responses instead? My prediction is that you will feel a whole lot better and much more liberated and inspired. This makes sense because you are thinking in terms of logical, reasonable thoughts, as opposed to nonsensical and self-preoccupied ones. You feel better because these new beliefs are part of the causes and conditions of feeling better. There is a central Buddhist idea that something comes into being because the right conditions have been created. Here, you have created the right conditions for inspiration, creative flow, and enlightened productivity. For me, that's the most elegant thing about this exercise – it not only leads to more positive feelings and higher levels of productivity, but it also replaces irrationality with statements that are much more wisdom-based and oriented to helping other sensitive beings like yourself.

5. Negative Emotions (After)

To the right of Rational and Other-Cherishing Responses is the last heading called Negative Emotions (After). In this column, the intensity of the negative emotions you identified in number 2 above are reevaluated. For example, in Figure 4.1 the original ratings under this column were: Anxiety, 90%; Guilt, 75%; Anger, 50%. After challenging the original self-cherishing, irrational thoughts, your negative emotions tend to diffuse and a calmer, balanced perspective is achieved. The new emotional levels are now: Anxiety, 10%; Guilt, 1%; Anger, 1%. Had you been doing this exercise, you would have succeeded in dramatically reducing your writing-defeating emotions.

Act Against Distorted Thinking

The late Albert Ellis, PhD, advocated the second technique to combat irrational beliefs, and it is simply this: *Act* against your cognitive distortions and your harmful emotions. This erodes the self-preoccupied nature of these thoughts, and if you act against them, with an enlightened motivation, the positive karmic consequences will be stronger. Recall once again that, within most Buddhist traditions, karmic consequences simply refer to the "footprints" left by your actions. These actions can even be thoughts or feelings. There is really not a lot to say about this technique except that it works because it proves that your thoughts are illogical, leading to feelings that are, therefore, inappropriate and often harmful in the sense that they dampen your enthusiasm and zest.

Let's use an example – the third belief we were working with in Figure 4.1 under Self-Cherishing, Irrational Thoughts – "I'm not going to write anything good anyway." Imagine if, in spite of having this belief, you force yourself to follow through with a planned two-hour writing session. You write well and you acknowledge that fact. Now you have concretely and behaviorally disproved your distorted belief! What more powerful method could there be for ridding yourself of self-preoccupied, irrational beliefs? Indeed, forcefully acting against your distorted beliefs about writing – or about anything else! – may be your most powerful tool for eradicating these beliefs. You are going to enjoy a level of freedom, bliss, self-compassion and compassion for others that you had never experienced previously, as well as infusing your creative endeavors with inspiration.

Let us look at another example "I must hang on to cherishing myself. Because if I don't, then I have lost myself, and I'm bound to be completely miserable." Imagine that you force yourself to act against this belief to test it, as you would test a scientific hypothesis. You force yourself to act in an other-cherishing manner, for example, meditating on generating loving-kindness toward people who are suffering, or you could do some volunteer work in a prison – teach Buddha Dharma to the inmates, or run a substance-abuse group.

You have made a decision and followed through with engaging altruistic, other-cherishing actions, even though it was your original belief that only self-cherishing would bring you happiness. Many people believe this. We could even say that this entirely faulty notion is the root of most, if not all, problems in the world, and also *the* nourishing root that holds you in a discontented life. But if your altruistic action brings you much happiness, then you have experientially disproved your original, self-cherishing idea. This would be an incredibly effective way to dispute the above self-preoccupied belief, validate an opposite belief experientially, and thus be more likely to act on this new, other-cherishing belief in the future – *because you have validated it through your own experience.* Through acting in any number of ways in which you focus on the needs of others you could invalidate the idea that only through looking out for yourself can you find happiness.

∽

A final word about the two techniques that have been presented thus far in this chapter. These two techniques are best used in combination with one another, although the exclusive use of one or the other will still produce positive changes. The Five-Column Technique works directly on changing self-cherishing and irrational thinking, and thereby changes harmful emotions and behavior – in your case, emotions and behavior about writing. Be sure to recall from previous chapters that self-cherishing simply refers to valuing yourself too much and being preoccupied with your self and your own needs and interests. In the West we might just call this self-centeredness! In the second technique, you first change your behavior by forcing yourself to act. For example, follow through on a planned writing session in spite of writing-defeating emotions such as anxiety.

Remember that you are writing mainly to benefit others, and this in itself will often help you to eliminate the negative emotions – they may immediately be replaced by bliss and happiness through changing your motivation. You often wind up with little or no anxiety and outstanding results. It often happens just this way for me when I have reminded myself why I am writing. My clients, whom I have coached in this manner, have reported similar experiences when reminding themselves to generate what is essentially an altruistic Buddhist motivation – transforming their writing session into spiritual practice.

At the end of the session, it is wise to dedicate the positivity or good karma accumulated to the benefit of all living beings – but more about that is in a later chapter. Let it suffice for now to say that the positivity that I have generated during these two hours of artistic endeavor, – I am giving away as a gift for everyone else so that they can share in my happiness and enjoyment. And since I am interconnected with everything else anyway, doesn't it make good sense for me to do this?

Use Rational Emotive Imagery (Longer Version)

The third powerful technique is called Rational Emotive Imagery (REI). This was pioneered by the psychiatrist Maxy C Maltsby, Jr. of the University of the Kentucky School of Medicine. This, and the technique that follows, are analogous to the concentrated and analytical meditation used within major Buddhist traditions. Practitioners will readily see parallels. In REI, you close your eyes and vividly imagine the Writing Situation or Event (WSE) or other Activating Event(s).

For example, at the beginning of this chapter, the WSE was simply the act of sitting down to write. In the REI, you simply visualize this and allow the painful emotions to emerge: the guilt about not having written yesterday, the anxiety that today's session isn't going to go well, and the depression because your project isn't going to go anywhere, anyway! I don't suggest you try to summon these emotions if they don't exist, however, we are assuming that this WSE *is* a problem for you. Go ahead and allow the guilt, anxiety, depression, and so forth to arise. Then, go over the rational, other-cherishing beliefs or enlightenment-oriented thoughts that you have developed in step 4 of the Five-Column Technique.

You are in essence *meditating* on the rational, other-cherishing beliefs that you have developed – your own enlightenment-driven thoughts! This produces a strengthening of these beliefs through pairing them with WSEs until they are automatically associated with the WSE. So, you wind up generating enlightenment-orientated reactions to the WSE – sitting down and writing – such as motivation, enthusiasm, exuberance, passion and creative fire. You go over them one by one in your REI process. I usually suggest you do this for about 20 minutes, but it may be as little as 5 minutes.

For instance, during your REI, while intensely visualizing the WSE, you would think, "Before the fact, how do I know that it is going to be *too* hard for me to sit and write for two hours? Even if it does prove to be difficult…" You will go through all the new, helpful beliefs in this manner. After 20 minutes you simply end your REI. With practicing this regularly, the rational, other-cherishing beliefs will *automatically* be associated with the WSE, and will no longer generate negative emotions. You will have replaced them with their opposites – with emotions that will fuel rather than diminish your creative efforts. This is a very powerful, experiential technique. Depending upon your memory, you may have to open your eyes during REI to read the rational, other-cherishing beliefs that have been generated in step 4 of the Five-Column Technique, but eventually you will have them memorized.

Now for the integration of REI with Buddha Dharma. People who meditate regularly within most of the Buddhist traditions will immediately see the similarities with concentrated and analytical meditation. Dr Maltsby has written that this technique works more quickly than prescription tranquilizers, and it's not habit-forming! You may experience so much benefit from this REI technique – thereby increasing your capacity to write – that it *does* become a regular habit. You can greatly diminish your tendency to generate self-defeating emotions to *any* Activating Event. Then the karmic consequences of your thoughts, behavior, and emotions will be positive. The strength will be even greater if you do REI not only to benefit yourself, but out of the altruistic aspiration to achieve enlightenment in order to guide all living beings to that state of supreme happiness and compassion.

Use Rational Emotive Imagery (Short Version)

The fourth and last technique that's going to be presented is REI, but Albert Ellis style. Dr Maltsby and the late Dr Albert Ellis, who pioneered cognitive behavioral therapy, were friends. Dr Ellis developed a version of REI that doesn't involve doing the Five-Column Technique first. You simply visualize what Ellis called an Activating Event. For example, let's say that giving a talk about your book is an Activating Event for you. You simply visualize yourself giving the talk, and allow yourself to feel anxiety, embarrassment or whatever the negative emotions. This is called *in vitro* exposure, which leads to desensitization – *in vitro* since the exposure is through your imagination as opposed to live exposure.

Controlled studies have validated the effectiveness of both methods. Desensitization occurs when you allow yourself to be flooded, as above, with an emotion like anxiety until you become incapable of generating anxiety about the Activating

Event. You are simply exposing yourself to the point that it no longer bothers you!

Individuals who have problems with anger can use this technique with regard to the Activating Event that typically makes them angry. Through this they can make themselves less vulnerable to anger over things about which they previously became enraged, and even physically or verbally aggressive. Obviously, these techniques can benefit not only your writing but concerning many Activating Events that you encounter. With a decreased capacity to become angry, you will avoid accumulation of the karmic negativities that would have occurred otherwise.

∽

Regarding all of the techniques in this chapter, if you practice them with the motivation to benefit yourself *and* others then they will be infinitely more beneficial than if you do them simply for yourself. This is the beauty of combining cognitive behavioral therapy with key insights from the Buddhist traditions – they are complementary, and you derive more benefit from their combination than you would from either of them separately. In the next chapter we are going to take a look at accepting yourself and cherishing others – regardless of writing – and how this accepting of yourself and cherishing of others enhances your ability to live and write.

Assignment 4.1:
Practicing the Five-Column Technique

You can use any project in which you're currently engaged as material for the Five-Column Technique. Start off by making plenty of copies of Worksheet 4.1. Then note your Writing Situation or Event in column one of the Five-Column Technique. Remember to write only the facts in this column – no interpretations! It is your interpretation of the facts and not the facts themselves that are leading to your depression, anxiety, guilt or whatever the writing-defeating emotions are.

In column two, number and write each of the negative emotions, and the extent to which you are feeling each of them, on a 1 to 99-percentage scale. In the third column, Self-Cherishing, Irrational Thoughts (Unenlightened Thoughts), write each of the thoughts that you are having about the Writing Situation or Event, just as illustrated in this chapter. These are your interpretations. They are leading directly to your writing-defeating emotions and delaying behavior.

Then, in column four, Rational and Other-Cherishing Responses (Enlightened Thoughts), write a new Enlightened Thought to substitute for each of the Unenlightened Thoughts in column three. Recall that Enlightened Thoughts are free of thinking distortions and reflect a balanced view regarding concern for self and concern for others. Here you are changing your interpretation of the Writing Situation or Event.

As you impose this interpretation, you will discover your guilt, anxiety, and depression shift dramatically in the direction of enthusiasm, inspiration, and zest about your project. And then you will write each of these new emotions in the fifth column called Negative Emotions (After) as well as rerating each of the emotions that you listed in column two.

The emotional transformation will take place just like tropical rain in a rainforest pouring down and cleansing all of the dirt and defilement from a Buddha statue, leaving it looking beautiful, shining, pristine and enlightened. Be sure to actually do this assignment and don't just read about it. While reading about it will help, reaping the true fruits of enlightenment is going to take the effort of actually doing the assignment, and even sometimes doing it repeatedly, every time you get into a funk in your writing or any other creative activity.

When you use this technique, don't just do it for your own benefit, but for the benefit of all living sensitive beings. Imagine that when you are doing the exercise, you are not only getting rid of your own self-defeating and painful emotions but with your enlightened motivation you are washing away the suffering of others as well. With the power of this technique and the power of this benevolent motivation, how can you not free yourself and even make progress toward freeing all others with whom you live interdependently?

Figure 4.1: Five-Column Technique Example Worksheet

Writing Situation or Event	Negative Emotions (Before)	Self-Cherishing, Irrational Thoughts	Rational and Other-Cherishing Responses	Negative Emotions (After)
I just sat down in my lounge chair with a cup of tea, a pen, and a notebook with plans to do a two-hour writing session	Anxiety, 90% Guilt, 75% Anger, 50%	1. "I missed my writing session yesterday, and I shouldn't have!" 2. "It's going to be too hard to sit here for two hours and write." 3. "I'm not going to write anything good anyway."	1. "Where is the law of the universe that states that I *should* have done my writing session yesterday? Nowhere is it written when and how much except in my head. It may have been better if I had done a writing session yesterday, but I don't become beyond redemption because I didn't, as my 'should statement' would suggest. Now let's get busy with today's session!" 2. "Before the fact, how do I know that it is going to be *too hard* for me to sit and write for two hours? Even if it does prove to be difficult, how could I prove that it would be *too hard*? I couldn't, because this would be equivalent to my trying to prove that it would be impossible for me to sit down and write for two hours. How illogical! For all I know, I may wind up finding fulfillment in this writing session – unless I try 'too hard' to make it a miserable session. It's possible that I might produce some writing during today's session that will be of enormous benefit. How can I know in advance? All I can do is sit down with an altruistic motivation and do today's writing session. Would I lack the compassion to ask any more than this from someone else – then why ask more than that from myself?" 3. "There's no way that I can know – before the fact – whether this is going to be a productive session in which something significant is produced, or not. Even if the session is less productive than I would have liked, the chances are that I would have produced something of value, especially with an altruistic motivation. Rather than making predictions, why not just get moving with an experimental attitude and see how the session turns out? Why not forget about myself, stop being preoccupied, realize my selflessness, and just flow rather than worrying about how well I'm flowing?"	Anxiety, 10% Guilt, 1% Anger, 1%

Worksheet 4.1: Five-Column Technique Form

Writing Situation or Event	Negative Emotions (Before)	Self-Cherishing, Irrational Thoughts	Rational and Other-Cherishing Responses	Negative Emotions (After)

Assignment 4.2:
Practicing Rational Emotive Imagery

Now that you have successfully completed *Assignment 4.1* – you have completed it, have you not? –you are now ready for practicing Rational Emotive Imagery. Your Enlightened Thoughts from Assignment 4.1 are the raw material for your Rational Emotive Imagery which, as you saw in this chapter, is very much like meditation. You are going to meditate on each one of your Enlightened Thoughts to strengthen it, and mentally connect it directly to the Writing Situation or Event that you started working on in *Assignment 4.1.*

Sit down in a comfortable place, with minimal noise or other distractions, a comfortable place in which you are able to concentrate well. For some people, this will be a quiet meditation room, and for others – like me! – it is often a busy coffee shop with music playing in the background and a lot of hustle-bustle going on around me. Close your eyes and vividly imagine the Writing Situation or Event that was linked with negative emotions for you. In the example in this chapter, for example, this involved simply the thought of sitting down and beginning your writing project.

Once you have the situation vividly in mind, go over each of the Enlightened Thoughts that you developed in Assignment 4.1. Go over them slowly and meditatively but with a little bit of passion to link them strongly with the formerly problematic Writing Situation or Event. Just as in the concentrated and analytical meditation that is practiced within a number of the Buddhists traditions, you are going to hold each thought in your mind as you picture your particular Writing Situation or Event.

I recommend that you do Rational Emotive Imagery in the manner described for 30 days in a row, up to, but not exceeding, 20 minutes a day. In other words, if you only have 5 minutes on a given day, that is fine. If you happen to miss a day, that's fine too.

Just resume your Rational Emotive Imagery the next day, without trying to make up for lost time in any way. You will notice that feelings of enthusiasm, zest, exuberance and motivation become automatically associated with your Writing Situation or Event from persistently doing Rational Emotive Imagery meditation.

When you practice your Rational Emotive Imagery, why not do it with the altruistic motivation of a bodhisattva? A bodhisattva is a person, like you, who is on the path to enlightenment. Therefore, when you do this assignment, do it not just for your own benefit, but imagine that you are doing it for the benefit of all other living beings as well. Since you are ultimately connected to everything and everyone else anyway, doesn't it make the most sense to do Rational Emotive Imagery with this motivation? At the very least, from doing this assignment persistently you are going to be a more calm, empathic, and productive person and more of a pleasure to be around for those intimates and others with whom you interact on a daily basis.

Chapter Five

LIBERATING YOUR WRITING AND LIVING THROUGH UNCONDITIONAL SERENITY

Can you have serenity when you are not being a prolific writer? Can you experience contentment even before you are a published writer? The answer, which I outline in this chapter, amounts to a resounding "Yes!" You can achieve this kind of serenity through having a good understanding of the eight worldly addictions, making progress toward overcoming them through the techniques that have already been discussed in the last two chapters, and from immersing yourself in an enlightenment-driven recovery group. Until you achieve full enlightenment, which is the perfect union of compassion and wisdom, you will be recovering from cyclic existence – which is fraught with suffering due to craving the objects of each of the worldly addictions – approval and status, for example. This cycle is traditionally referred to in Tibetan Buddhist scriptures as samsara.

The Eight Worldly Addictions

You will attain unconditional serenity when you stop following your craving for the substance of the eight worldly addictions, traditionally known by Tibetan Buddhists as the eight worldly dharmas. They are the following:

- being happy when acquiring material things
- being unhappy when not acquiring material things
- wanting to be happy
- not wanting to be unhappy
- wanting to hear interesting sounds
- not wanting to hear uninteresting sounds
- wanting praise
- not wanting criticism

When you stop making your "contentment" dependent upon indulging in the eight worldly addictions, then you will have attained unconditional serenity. Let's examine them two at a time, because in traditional Dharma books they are presented in pairs.

Addiction to Material Acquisitions

So, the first pair that we will look at is, "being happy when acquiring material things, and being unhappy when not acquiring material things". In your writing and your life, this addiction makes your serenity dependent upon acquiring material things, and also on not losing material positions. This leaves you very vulnerable.

From the standpoint of contemporary cognitive behavioral therapy, it's actually probably fine to be dissatisfied if you don't get that top-notch publishing house for your book, or if you lose your contract with an excellent publisher. Then, you won't be able to acquire some of the material things that your advance royalties would have enabled you to afford. But, the secret is to not *need* the contract in the first place, and to not *need* to keep it once you have it. It's fine and healthy to have a desire for attaining something, and a desire to keep it once you have it, – this will lead to your being motivated to fulfill the obligations to your contract concerning the publication of your book. But, when you slip into *needing* material things, then you've slipped into addiction.

So, avoid needing and thus addiction to material acquisitions, and stick with *preferring* these acquisitions, and then you'll be moving towards unconditional serenity. In other words, use a self-statement like, "I'd like that new Armani suit or that Versace dress, but I can be completely serene without it, because I know in my heart of hearts that I only prefer it, and never, never *need* it!" Perhaps with a mindset that's progressed even further toward enlightenment, you wouldn't even prefer it, because you'd already have so much compassion, bliss, wisdom, and serenity that you'd be indifferent to the Versace dress yourself. What would cause you to experience even more sublime happiness would be to see someone else enjoying it.

Addiction to Happiness

The second worldly addiction pairing, as it is traditionally stated is, "wanting to be happy, and not wanting to be unhappy". Well, this one seems innocent enough on the surface. Who doesn't want to be happy? And the way that it is actually stated above is probably healthy, and not an addiction. But you, along with most other humans, often go to the extreme of believing that they *need* to be happy, and *must* not be unhappy. With these needs and musts, you go into unhealthy addiction. Like other addictions, being addicted to happiness, and believing that you must not be unhappy – that you absolutely couldn't stand this under any conditions – leaves you very vulnerable. In psychotherapy, this is called "low frustration tolerance." This is a fancy way of saying that tolerating any short-term unhappiness or frustration is not possible for you. If this is the case, how are you going to tolerate the short-term frustration and momentary diminution of happiness in the here and now that are associated with doing today's writing session, which is going to lead to the completion of your manuscript, article, or story? You won't, if you are addicted to happiness!

Addiction to happiness will be as hobbling to you in your writing, life, and relationships as addiction to approval, success, food, acquiring material things, or anything else. Also, think about how self-cherishing it is for you to constantly be concerned about how happy you are. So, it's best for you to stick to a rational, enlightenment-oriented self-statement that goes something like this: "Yes, I prefer happiness, and I don't particularly like unhappiness! But, I can tolerate some unhappiness and sometimes even some fairly heavy doses of unhappiness and frustration for the purpose of benefiting others. For example, through the completion of a manuscript that is going to be of help to a lot of people. Paradoxically, with my belief that I can tolerate unhappiness and that it's acceptable, I will wind up being happy and joyful because of the resilient mindset that I will develop with my writing."

Once you have made a substantial amount of progress toward complete enlightenment, you may even be beyond the level of preferring to be happy, and may simply find yourself being happy through vicariously experiencing the happiness of others. In fact, enlightened happiness is experiencing happiness in and through the happiness of others, because of knowing that their happiness is inseparable from your own!

Addiction to Sensual Pleasures

For this addiction, traditional texts speak only of sounds. Specifically, this pairing of worldly addictions, as they often appear in Dharma books are, "wanting to hear interesting sounds, and not wanting to hear uninteresting sounds". This makes me think of all pleasures that we experience with our other senses such as taste, sight, smell, and touch. We want to experience good tastes and don't want to experience unpleasant ones. We want to look at people who are adorned in the best designer clothes and don't want to look at people who are dressed in shabby clothes, and so forth. Once again, this addiction leads to you to be very, very vulnerable because you're not going to be serene unless you have whatever sensual pleasure or pleasures that you so desperately want – in other words, that you desperately *need*. You have this addiction if you *need* to have sensual pleasure, and absolutely *must* avoid sensual displeasure at all costs.

Think of how many people are enslaved because of falling into this category. They experience life as being totally void of freedom and pleasure precisely because they are so strongly addicted to pleasure! With this addiction, from where are you going to muster the discipline to be a prolific writer, not to mention living life in a wholesome and robustly virtuous manner, in which you move away from the cycle of suffering and toward the bliss of enlightenment? Better to do away with this addiction completely, yes? Stick with a rational, enlightenment-driven motivation for sensual pleasures which comes in the form of preferences for certain sensual pleasures, as long as they are of a wholesome nature.

This is in line with the thinking of the Buddha that the path of complete asceticism is not helpful, and will not help you to make progress toward enlightenment. Nor will it help you to make progress toward writing and living in a creatively inspired, passionate manner. So, stick with a self-statement such as this, "I like sensual pleasures, provided they help and don't harm myself and others. But, they are never, never *needed* for me to be serene and content. In fact, my belief that I do need them will keep me in a constant cycle of addiction, and away from experiencing much enjoyment. Further, I won't complete chapters, manuscripts, book proposals, articles, and the like, which could help many people, if I'm thinking that sensual pleasure is required in big doses, all of the time. I'll probably wind up losing perspective and chase after unwholesome sensual pleasures, which will have negative karmic consequences, and affect my lives in a negative manner. So, I'll stay away from asceticism, but I'll also stay away from the other extreme of addiction to sensual pleasures!"

As you make thoroughgoing progress toward the perfect union of compassion and wisdom which is enlightenment, you'll find yourself becoming indifferent to mundane pleasures because of the state of supreme serenity and bliss that will have stabilized for you.

Addiction to Approval

The last pair of worldly addictions involves approval. In classic Buddhist texts, this pair is often mentioned like this: "wanting praise, and not wanting criticism". It's fairly obvious how this would be dysfunctional for a writer, not to mention someone who wants to live in a state of serenity and contentment. This is especially true because, as with the other addictions that have been discussed, most people take this one a step further and transform it into a diabolical, dire *need*. It's completely paralyzing to your writing if you have this supposed need. It will be extremely difficult if not impossible for you to produce much work of an original, inventive, authentic nature. Why? Because being original involves taking a risk of being criticized. And if you have this dire, diabolical, crippling *need* to be praised and to avoid criticism, how are you going to be able to take the risks involved in being original and authentic?

What is worse, no matter what you produce, some people will still criticize you, and this criticism will lead you to suffer tremendously. Will it really be the criticism and absence of praise that is leading to your suffering? No, it won't! Instead, it will be your dire need for approval – your addiction to approval. So, it's better to keep a *preference* for receiving praise and approval, and avoiding criticism. In this way you'll enjoy praise, and criticism will leave you a little frustrated and annoyed, but not devastated. Therefore, use a serenity-oriented self-statement that goes something like the following, "There is no reason why I *must* have praise, and avoid criticism. I can rationally prefer to receive praise, or positive criticism, and not receive negative criticism, but that is it.

"This never relates to the worth of my writing, and it certainly doesn't relate to my worth as a person. In fact, if my writing is lavishly praised or harshly criticized, neither relates one iota to my worth as a person or my capacity for serenity, because I have unconditional serenity from not being addicted to approval!"

As you proceed even further toward enlightenment, you will become indifferent to approval altogether, and simply and selflessly experience bliss in the process of living and writing for the benefit of living beings, and their environment.

Techniques for Overcoming Worldly Addictions

So, don't be driven toward these eight worldly addictions, change them to preferences, and ultimately surrender the preferences. When you succeed at this, you will have attained unconditional serenity and contentment. The Mahayana Buddhist tradition calls this nirvana – the cessation of suffering and the attainment of peace. However, the ultimate goal of the Mahayana tradition is complete, perfect enlightenment for the sake of all sentient beings. But unconditional serenity is a good intermediate goal, don't you think? Achieving this state in a lifetime will require you to stop wasting this precious human life that you have – then you can avoid re-entering samsara in your next rebirth. Your continuation, your subtle wisdom essence, is what is transmitted into your next life according to Sogyal Rinpoche, Gehlek Rinpoche and other masters from the Tibetan Buddhist tradition. The main point, however, is that you can free yourself from samsara – the cycle of suffering, which has existed since beginningless time – and enter unconditional serenity by overcoming the eight worldly addictions. Simply by not chasing the eight worldly addictions, you will stop generating negative karma and negative karma is the cause for the continuation of suffering.

Don't take my word for it, and don't take the word of Shakyamuni Buddha (the historical Buddha who attained enlightenment some 2,500 years ago), because with these techniques you're going to do it!

This leads to the first technique for your gaining self-acceptance, other-cherishing, and unconditional serenity, regardless of how much you write, how well you write, or how your work is received – whether with praise or with criticism. Let's say you have the following belief: "My writing *must* be accepted lavishly by my readers for me to be happy." Well, test this belief out. Like a good scientist, check your hypothesis. Because after all, your belief is not a fact – it is but a hypothesis! You're going to be using the technique from Chapter Four called, "acting against your irrational, self-cherishing beliefs".

Go through with a number of writing sessions without showing anyone what you have written. If you experience happiness during these sessions or afterwards, you will have disproved the belief because you will have written, and experienced happiness independent of anyone else's opinion. You simply did your writing and experienced happiness in the process, and that was that.

You will begin to renounce the eight worldly addictions as they relate to your writing by doing experiments such as this. The effect of these experiments will be very powerful because they involve experiential learning. In addition, if you fully accept yourself during these sessions and write with a benevolent, other-cherishing motivation, you are likely to experience serenity that is sublime; yet no one will have praised or criticized your writing. It may be a sublime serenity like one that has never known suffering, because it will be serenity that is a by-product of having renounced the eight worldly addictions. It will be unconditional serenity. You can experience this more and more in aspects of your life outside of writing, and thus successively approximate cutting the craving and the attachment that binds you to the eight worldly addictions, and thus to samsara and suffering.

Remember you can use the Five-Column Technique and Rational Emotive Imagery to remove your self-cherishing, irrational beliefs that cause attachment to and craving of the eight worldly addictions. In adapting the Five-Column Technique, let's say that the Writing Situation or Event (WSE) is that an article you wrote received criticism from some of your colleagues. Briefly write down the details of this in column one of the Five-Column Technique (use a notebook or photocopy *Worksheet 4.1* from the previous chapter). Write down each of the afflictive emotions that you are experiencing about this criticism in column two, giving each emotion a percentage rating. In the third column, write each of your irrational, self-cherishing beliefs that are the basis of your afflictive emotions, which are keeping you in samsara, and gloating in the eight worldly addictions – in this case, not wanting criticism. Don't forget that can you easily identify these beliefs by asking yourself, about the WSE, "What does this situation mean to me, and why is it upsetting to me?" By asking yourself this question, you will be able to uproot your underlying self-cherishing, irrational belief, which might go somewhat like, "My colleagues must think highly of my work – if they don't, then I'm incompetent as a professional, and worthless as a person." With this belief, no wonder their criticism bothers you so much!

Fourth, you can label your cognitive distortions, and then write a more rational, other-cherishing belief to replace each belief in column three. Finally, re-rate each of the afflictive emotions from column two – often their intensity will go down to zero or near zero. Then, after you do Rational Emotive Imagery (REI), your ratings will almost always go to zero, and positive feelings will emerge and take the place of the negative ones.

This is wonderful – and ironic – because the external situation has not changed at all! Your paper was criticized by several of your colleagues. That reality hasn't changed. But, by having generated rational, other-cherishing beliefs, and then practicing them experientially through REI, your afflictive emotions have been eliminated and have been replaced by empowering ones. These healthy feelings can involve enthusiasm regarding going on with your work. You will have made progress toward reducing your attachment to the eight worldly addictions, and thus toward reaching unconditional serenity.

Unconditional serenity is defined as a consciousness immune to generating afflictive emotions from activating events – that's what makes it truly *unconditional*. Of course, to continue movement toward attaining the omniscient state of a Buddha, there are additional requirements, such as bodhimind, or the altruistic motivation to seek enlightenment so as to best help other living beings through vast wisdom and compassion. But you will be *moving toward* the actualization of your buddha-nature, in living and writing with unconditional serenity.

You can also practice REI, Albert Ellis style, as described in Chapter Four. In doing so, you would visualize the WSE for a given number of minutes each day, and you will habituate to it as being an Activating Event that has the potential of igniting afflictive emotions within you. For many people, a combination of all of these techniques is of the most benefit – the Five-Column Technique, both types of REI, and acting against your irrational, self-cherishing beliefs so as to experientially disprove them.

In the next chapter, we are going to look at how freedom from attachment to the eight worldly addictions and mundane desire will enable you to focus on being process-oriented in your writing and in your life.

Assignment 5.1:
Start Your Own Enlightenment-Driven Recovery Group

Go ahead and implement the Buddha Dharma and cognitive behavioral techniques that I have just reviewed to put a damper on the strength of your worldly addictions to happiness, material acquisitions, approval, and sensual pleasure. However, these addictions are cunning, baffling, and powerful, so you're going to need more than that to fully release yourself from their hold, enter nirvana, and ultimately gain full enlightenment. You are going to need the assistance of a recovery group. Recovery from what, you may be asking? Your recovery is going to be from samsara, which is the relative state of suffering in which most of us exist. And it is these four addictions that keep you bound to a life of unstable serenity.

You can't get out of these addictions completely on your own, as isolation is a breeding ground in which addictions flourish. The problem is that an enlightenment-driven "recovery from samsara" group doesn't exist, so it is up to you, my dear reader, to start one! This does not have to be a big group of over 30 people, although it may turn out that way as the enlightenment movement catches hold. You are going to, in essence, start an Enlightenment Anonymous group, where the sole purpose is to break free from the cycle of suffering, and through to enlightenment.

You can think of Alcoholics Anonymous as a prototype. There, people are working together for the common purpose of staying sober. They meet together, discuss common topics, read common books, and have slogans, which are shared by everyone. The only requirement for membership is the desire to stop drinking. The only requirement for membership to Enlightenment Anonymous is the desire to overcome the worldly addictions, and thus achieve freedom from suffering. You can just start off by meeting with just one other person with whom you share this aim. You are free to work out the details on your own, but some general guidelines follow.

Start by meeting once or twice a week for an hour or so. As reading material, a good place to start may be the Suggested Reading section at the end of this book. You might want to start by agreeing upon a book with your discussion partner or partners. Then, one possible format for the meeting would be to start at the beginning of the book, and take turns reading from it. After each person is finished reading, then time can be opened up for comments. These can take the form of insights gained from the reading and how it can be applied, either in everyday living, or to a specific problem that someone has.

Another format would involve a person who is "chairing" the meeting choosing a topic with which everyone in the group has a working knowledge, such as transcendent generosity. Then, each person in the group can share what this means to them personally, how they use it for self-improvement, and what beneficial results have been obtained.

Alternatively, an hour-long meeting could begin with concentrated meditation, where everyone in the group meditates for the first 20 minutes on a particular theme, such as compassion. Then, each person can share the realizations gained from the concentrated meditation, as well as how their bodhisattva practice of compassion impacts their everyday life.

A final possible format is the "lead" meeting, which is frequently used in recovery groups. Using this format, one person would give a lead, which means that they would share with the entire group what their life was like before they discovered the Dharma, what happened that caused them to come into contact with it and take it to heart, and how their life changed in terms of increased serenity, improved relationships, and greater vocational satisfaction as a result.

Any of these recovery formats bring Buddha Dharma to life in a very real, personal way. Some readers may even wish to develop steps and traditions, which are different in content from, but analogous to the steps and traditions in Alcoholics Anonymous and other twelve-step recovery groups. I think it's no coincidence that step twelve of these groups involves "having had a spiritual awakening", to which I would apply the term "enlightenment".

If you don't already belong to one, you might begin this assignment by joining a Buddha Dharma organization that is already in existence in your community. For example, I live in the Midwest, and am a member of Jewel Heart, which has centers close to where I live and is led by Gehlek Rimpoche, who studied under the same teachers as His Holiness the Fourteenth Dalai Lama. My point is that by joining such an organization, you will be able to derive substantial spiritual sustenance from it, as well as connecting yourself with people who can become members of your own Enlightenment Anonymous group.

Don't jump in and start frantically recruiting people, or the organization may begin to recruit support to oust you from it! Instead, and in the spirit of the tradition, get involved in the organization and let your experiences teach you how best to proceed with your own enlightenment-driven agenda. Furthermore, attending retreats is a fantastic way of meeting other like-minded people. These are frequently advertised in magazines for practitioners such as Buddhadharma, Mandala, Shambhala Sun, and Tricycle, or may be organized by the spiritual director or senior students of the Buddha Dharma center or other spiritual organization to which you belong.

As usual, the spiritual approach of your group does not have to be Buddha Dharma specifically. Any enlightenment-oriented outlook will do, with this being defined as wanting to overcome worldly attachments and addictions that lead to suffering, gaining greater compassion, and increasing wisdom in how best to put this compassion into practice. Most of the world's

main spiritual traditions certainly embody these values,
expressed in a unique way and through a unique cultural and
historical prism. Each of these traditions has its own historical as
well as mythical personalities in which common truths are
expressed and transmitted.

Chapter Six

WRITING IN THE PRESENT MOMENT

This chapter truly comes from the bottom of my heart. It is my philosophy of why the *process* of writing is the most important part of writing. When I think of the word "process", I think of it as the most important aspect of how I live and write.

In 1991, I became a social-work practitioner, specializing in the difficulties pertaining to severely mentally disabled adults. My clients often talked about how they would be happy or satisfied when they got a job, found a meaningful relationship, developed better work skills or social skills, better tolerated stress and achieved a stable housing situation. Fine so far! But what about enjoying the process of getting to these goals? Similarly, I often stubbornly insisted to myself that things would be fine after I finished my Ph.D. and embarked on a full-time career of teaching and writing. But what about enjoying my life in the meantime? What I had yet to learn was that these *ends* were important, but so was the process of getting to them, especially since that's where all my time was being spent!

This is the core of what I now tell my audiences of writers, potential writers, and mental-health professionals: have goals, and even fairly challenging ones, yet become passionately absorbed in and thoroughly enjoy the process of getting to them.

Discovering the Process-Orientation

One of the most important people who taught me how to practice effective psychotherapy, particularly cognitive behavioral therapy, was David D Burns, MD. He reintroduced me to this idea of having a process-orientation in a formal capacity, because as an undergraduate, I had essentially invented the idea on my own and even wrote a paper about it. I called it "The Fiction of the Future Cycle". In other words, what I argued is that people tolerate a miserable present existence because of their fiction, or questionable assumption, that they're bound to be happy when they achieve some goal in the future. They become temporarily happy, but just set another goal to replace the old one, and then they are hardly ever happy until they reach this new one. And on and on you go, in a vicious cycle of unhappiness, that doesn't end. Not a very happy picture, and in fact, not a bad description of what Tibetan Buddhist's call samsara, or the endless cycle of suffering.

So, go ahead and liberate yourself from this cycle, in your writing and your life, by developing a process-orientation, which is what you're going to learn how to do in this chapter after a little more background. So read on!

David Burns' reintroduction of this idea into my life – I had literally forgotten the notion as I relentlessly drove myself toward my goals – was important for me because at that time when I was sitting with my psychotherapy clients, I was almost exclusively focused on the outcome of our sessions. Paradoxically, because of this outcome-orientation, I wasn't getting very good outcomes! Now that I look back, the outcome focus was based mainly on my self-preoccupation. I had to be the one influencing the client, as if I were the most important element in the client-therapist relationship. Instead of focusing on helping the client, which would be cherishing another, I was always concerned with how well I was doing.

The agency where I worked required us to have clients complete a Brief Mood Survey at the beginning of each therapy session and also at the end of sessions to determine if the client had experienced a reduction in afflictive emotions during our time together. The Brief Mood Survey was thus a way of determining how effective the session had been – what the outcome was. Again, I wanted to be the clinician who was getting the best results, which shows still further my preoccupation with my performance – with myself! – during the sessions. With this orientation, the sessions were stressful for me, and weren't decreasing the stress level of the clients in an optimal manner either.

When Dr Burns reintroduced me to the idea of having a process-orientation, I followed his advice to the letter. What happened was remarkable. When I stopped focusing so much on the outcomes of sessions, and just focused on being of benefit to the client in the here and now, my results dramatically improved! The clients' scores on the Brief Mood Survey, concerning their afflictive emotions (anger, anxiety, depression, and guilt) became dramatically lower by the end of the sessions than they had been when I had an outcome-orientation. Also, my clients began to comment in a much more positive way about their sessions, and they visibly appeared to benefit from the sessions. They showed not only a reduction in their afflictive emotions, but a decrease in their self-injurious and other harmful behaviors as well. The sessions also became much more rewarding and enjoyable for me. I was also modeling a process-orientation for the clients, as opposed to being driven to accomplish an end product. This process-orientation actually contained the best of both worlds, enjoyment of working with clients combined with excellent outcomes.

I began to explicitly teach this orientation to clients, whether they were homemakers, business people, writers, artists, and even spiritual practitioners of various religious traditions. When they switched to a process-orientation, their afflictive emotions and harmful behaviors became markedly reduced, and their altruistic inclinations and positive emotions increased. Some clients had difficulty with attaining a process-orientation, and I will discuss remedies later in this chapter. When I became a supervisor and a therapist trainer, I found that almost all the therapists with whom I worked initially had an outcome-orientation. Partly because of this, they suffered from performance anxiety, feelings of inadequacy, and were relatively ineffective with their clients. When I helped them move to a process-orientation and an empathic orientation toward helping in the here and now, in the process, they became much more effective and content clinicians.

In a sense, they renounced their concern about needing to produce excellent outcomes and needing to not produce bad outcomes. So they achieved a degree of liberation, by renouncing two of the eight worldly addictions that we visited in the previous chapter. They also became less self-preoccupied and more cherishing of others, as my clients and I myself had done previously.

Seeing the tremendous benefits of the process-orientation in all of these avenues and with all of these different people, I reflected on the fact that it produces such good results. Would it work with writing in terms of making the process both more enjoyable and, at the same time, lead to those well-constructed powerful sentences that I wanted to see on the pages of my books and articles? And the answer that I soon discovered with experimenting with the process-orientation in my writing was not only an exuberant "yes", but also a triumph "like magic!" This orientation of focusing on enjoying and completely absorbing myself in the process of producing manuscripts worked like magic not only for me, but for my clients as well. When they stopped needing to have well-constructed, powerful sentences which embodied their own style and just focused on the process of producing these sentences and enjoying it, their work began to flow. And flow like water, as opposed to cement!

A particular graduate student immediately comes to mind.

With one session of process-orientation coaching, he went from taking 30 or 40 hours to write a 10-page paper to doing the same length paper – and a much better, more lively piece of work – in 6 or 7 hours. Virtually everyone who was open to switching to a process-orientation experienced a similar, dramatic liberation.

So, be open to giving it a try yourself! To aid you in the process, I'm going to share with you some techniques to help you to switch from more of an outcome-orientation to a process-orientation.

Switching to a Process-Orientation

1. Free yourself of the eight worldly addictons

Remember that eight addictions (*see* Chapter Six) really boil down to four – material acquisitions, happiness, sensual pleasures, and approval. The more attached you remain to these, the more you will remain in a stressful outcome-orientation, not only in your writing, but even in the more important art of living as well. So, continue to put into practice the techniques recommended for subduing these. This will lead to unconditional serenity.

With this type of supreme serenity, you can't be in a stressful outcome-orientation. The two are simply incompatible! And in addition to the plethora of cognitive behavioral therapy techniques discussed in the last chapter, the enlightenment-driven recovery group that you are starting will help to really unglue you from these addictions, and help you to flow blissfully in a productive process-orientation in your arts of living and writing.

2. Be mindful and aware

The next kernel of advice simply involves being mindful and aware. In other words, if you're feeling stressed and tense, notice this! Become aware of it, and develop the habit of checking in with yourself. If you are feeling pressure, assume that you are putting pressure on yourself – no one else is doing it to you! Assume also that you are in an outcome-oriented mode. You have a certain outcome in your mind, you are fixated on it, and you are thinking that you *must* achieve it.

You might have in mind your fabulous completed book, and being interviewed about it on National Public Radio. This may be inspiring to daydream about, but it's going to be counterproductive with respect to crunching out sentences in today's writing session. So, first of all, let go of the *must* about the outcome and change it to a preference. Then, stop focusing on it all together, and simply focus yourself back on your writing task at hand, such as finishing today's writing session. You will usually feel immediate relief and start to get back into a state of creative absorption and flow (which is another way of saying process-orientation).

3. Mark your time

Remember from previous chapters that you are writing or revising for a maximum of two hours on any given day. In accord with this, put your time-keeping device in a place where you can view it at all times during your session. Then, make a real effort to keep yourself "in" this two-hour block of time as much as possible, during your session. Only think about what you're writing about – not the outcome – either of the session or your long-term objective, such as your published book or its level of success in the marketplace, or your article or assignment. Whenever your thinking does go to something else, simply bring it back to the two-hour block of time in which you are currently working.

As far as your time-keeping device itself, a clock with a second hand and minute hand can be very effective for most writers. For those who are a bit less conventional, something like an egg timer can be very effective. You can set a typical egg timer for a maximum of 60 minutes. But if you are someone who has trouble focusing, you can set it 3 times for 40 minutes each, and take a brief break after the first two times that the timer goes off. Then, you only have to be "in" the process for a relatively short period of time, with each setting. And when the egg timer goes off the third time, your 120 minutes of writing or revising is completed for the day. The effect of these simple strategies can seem almost miraculous in terms of how much they can reduce your stress, and increase your focus and productivity.

4. Transfer your state

By "transferring your state" I don't mean moving to a different state if you are a reader who lives in the United States! What I do mean is to transfer your complete mind-body situation from an outcome-orientation to more of a process-orientation. So, do this by thinking of some activity in which you naturally get yourself into a blissful, flowing, process-oriented state of mind. It can be anything – camping, hiking, fine dining, reading, sex, hand-holding, looking at the ocean, painting? Close your eyes and vividly imagine yourself doing the activity in which you naturally go into a state of flow. Really, really get there by thinking about what you are seeing, hearing, smelling, touching, feeling, and even tasting. Once you've really captured the sense of being in flow, stay in that mind-body state as you go into your writing session. Focus intently on bringing this mind-body state of flow into your writing session. You can do this because you can use your nervous system in many ways. It's not necessary to get into a tense, outcome-state just because you have started writing. Stay with the process. You can use your nervous system to be in a state of flow and peak perform-ance during your writing sessions, and transferring your state is but one way to access flow. If halfway through your session you find yourself uptight with your writing not flowing very well, simply repeat the technique of transferring your state.

5. Visualize your audience

This strategy involves seeing the actual audience for whom you are writing. For example, I had difficulty giving into a process-orientation about writing this chapter about a process-orientation! A state of flow did not come immediately. So, I asked myself, "What do you really want to say to your audience – at retreats for writers, for instance – about the process-orientation and why it's important for them?" As soon as I thought about it this way, my writing began to go in the direction of flow. Thinking about my audience, and what would help them, anchored me in the present moment.

Along similar lines, it doesn't hurt at all to have a photograph or some other visual representation of the audience within view during your sessions. Glance at it at times when you become stuck, and you will find yourself quickly becoming unstuck. You may invent other ways to anchor yourself in the here and now. But seeing myself as actually saying the words to the target audience is always a sure-fire way for me to achieve a process-orientation, and it also rarely fails for my writer-clients and writers with whom I am often in conversation.

6. Compartmentalize

My final piece of advice to you is this – put your writing sessions in a separate compartment from anything else in your life. As a rule of thumb, don't think about your writing when you're not in the midst of writing or revision, and don't think about outside things when you are in the midst of a writing session. You can't follow this rule perfectly because you're not a robot, and because you don't want to make yourself robotic; so it's best that you don't follow this rule 100 per cent. But in general, you will find that when you are in a state of flow and process-orientation during your sessions, you are completely absorbed and aren't thinking about anything else. Similarly, when you are in engaged in love-making in the most exquisite manner possible, you are completely there and aren't thinking about anything or anyone else – you are totally in the moment. The exact same thing applies to your writing.

When your writing is of this nature, you will find the same type of blissful, creative, explosive insights coming forth as if you were love-making with the written word – and you, in fact, will be doing just that! When you discover yourself thinking about something else during a writing session, simply and gently bring your mind back to the session, and the flow in your writing will be a natural result of this mental shift, or return to mindfulness. You can apply this same compartmentalization philosophy – as long as it's in a non-compulsory manner – to practically all aspects of your life such as cooking, driving, reading, being with your significant other, meditating, traveling and (as above), exquisite love-making.

Along with this compartmentalization theme, I try not to think very much about writing outside of scheduled writing sessions when it is best to be focusing on whatever else I am doing. A lot of writers obsessively think about their writing almost all the time. I don't think that this does their mental health much good. If we were to interview their life mates, I bet that they would confirm the negative effect on relationships by this obsessive approach. What is most important, from the point of view of producing brilliant, inspiring sentences, is that this approach does not improve your writing, either! So, if it doesn't help your enjoyment, and it doesn't help your relationships, and it doesn't even help your writing, why bother with obsessing about your writing all the time? The *Writing Time Log*, which is described in another chapter, is a great visual representation, which can remind you to compartmentalize your writing time, and make it distinct from other parts of your life.

There is but one exception to this rule. Occasionally, sometimes even daily, you may come up with an insight for an entire book, story or article. Or you may come up with the solution to a key problem about how you're going to handle finishing a chapter in your book. Or it will suddenly dawn on you what the ten key points arc that are going to be the foundation of the next chapter in your book!

Well, you don't want to let these huge windows of creative opportunity close before you capture their essence. So, carry around a notebook and, as soon as possible after you have the idea, jot it down. Make a good enough record so that in a later writing session, you can recall that creative window into which you had a view. Try to do this in the very setting in which you had the insight, because trying to do so in another setting may not allow as spectacular a view, and maybe not even any ability to see. Certain settings will evoke insights for you, and you may not even know what it is about the place that brings about a moment of genius. So, if at all possible, jot down some good notes right there and then – this is raw material that you will plug into a later writing session.

It's sometimes inconvenient, and there is sometimes some angst involved in the above, for me anyway. Other writers really enjoy these moments of illumination, and making notes about them. But the point is, if you don't make this one definite exception to the compartmentalization rule, you're simply going to miss collecting the "unrefined diamonds" that can be taken into later sessions and cleaned, cut, and polished to be sold at an unfathomable price.

ॐ

Now that your writing sessions are so productive that they can be compared to harvesting and cutting diamonds, you are ready for the next chapter, in which we are going to discuss using this precious human life of yours in the most favorable way possible!

Chapter Seven

USING YOUR PRECIOUS HUMAN LIFE TO THE FULLEST

You have learned about cognitive distortions and root delusions and have begun to make headway at improving your life and your writing. You have made some good progress in overcoming the eight worldly addictions, thereby making unconditional serenity and a joyous process-orientation possible in your writing and your life. It is all a process anyway, so why not fully embrace it and fully live in the present moment? And now that you have made this headway, you're ready to really recognize how positive your situation is, and what great opportunities lie at your fingertips.

Recognizing Your Very Auspicious Situation

Why is your situation so favorable, and why should you not waste time and fail to actualize the opportunities that are before you? Here are the reasons. And really read carefully because it's possible you won't ever read or hear them again, and at the same time it's possible that in this section are the most important words you will ever hear or read.

From the Tibetan Buddhist perspective, your existence is

completely wonderful and amazing because having what the Tibetan's call a "human rebirth" is extremely rare compared to other types of births and rebirths. His holiness the Fourteenth Dalai Lama, the most famous representative of this tradition, has written that a human rebirth is as rare as this example illustrates. Let's say a turtle came to the surface of the ocean – and it can rise to the surface of any of the oceans on earth – only once every 1,000 years. Now, let's say that in one of these oceans there is a lasso, about the size of the tire of a car, on the top of the water. What are the chances that the turtle's head would come through the surface of that lasso? Not very great, correct! Well, the Dalai Lama says that the rareness of a human rebirth is about as rare as that! So, continuing with this perspective, you'd best put much effort into fulfilling the great potential that your human existence affords you. This is the potential to become a Buddha, which is another way of saying, "fully enlightened".

We have still not upped the stakes all the way with the lasso analogy, because there are even more reasons why your particular human life is so precious! In addition to your human rebirth, you have connected with the teachings of the Buddha – even if through only having read this one book – and these are the technologies that you need to make full use of your human birthright to obtain enlightenment. It could be that you have connected with another of the great spiritual traditions, such as Christianity. So once again you will have connected to teachings which are capable of being put into practice by you, and leading you to enlightenment, although the preferable analogous term in the Christian tradition would be "salvation".

So you have attained this human life, you have connected with enlightenment-oriented technologies or teachings, and that's still not all! If you are reading this book, you have financial resources and some leisure time to learn about these spiritual technologies and put these into practice in your life. You live in a free, open society in which you are not tyrannically repressed and unable to put the technologies you are learning into practice. You presumably have adequate food, water, health care, supportive relationships – and the list could go on – and all of these are very auspicious conditions for living and writing in the fullest manner possible. So, don't waste this opportunity – one that's so marvelous that it's almost overwhelming when you really contemplate it.

Notice I'm not saying that you *must* take full advantage of this opportunity, or that you *should* or *must* do so every single minute. As has been discussed previously, such irrational thinking will lead you to feel unnecessary tension and constriction of your creativity. So it's best to stick with an enlightenment-oriented philosophy such as, "I know that my human life is very precious and I will strive to use my time as best I can to achieve my potential for enlightenment, and help as many beings as I can. And I'll even enjoy the process of moving toward and ultimately attaining enlightenment – why not enjoy the journey as well?"

Westerners Don't Use Time Well

There was a great Tibetan master who spent some time in the United States. When he returned to his residence in India, he was asked by one of his Western colleagues, "What was your most important observation about Western culture?" The master's answers caused his colleague to do a lot of reflection, for the master replied, "In the West, people waste time." Even economists talk about how people don't use time efficiently in the United States, because although we take fewer vacations by far than many European countries, our productivity rates are lower, and many of our products are of lower quality. The master wasn't even talking about this type of thing, however, because he was referring to spirituality. For example, while a person may be awake for 18 hours a day, virtually none of that time is spent in pursuing greater spiritual development – the development that would lead to enlightenment, and service to other sensitive beings. From the point of view of *Write for Your Lives*, I'm going to discuss three ways in which we Westerners waste a lot of time.

Writing Trashy Fiction

Unfortunately, when we write, we don't write for our lives – we write trashy fiction instead. You might ask what's so bad about an entertaining novel, or even reading a "fuck book" (as one of my professors humorously referred to them) once in a while. Well, in a sense you are only *reading* about what Tibetan Buddhist's call "sexual misconduct", and you aren't actually *doing* this. True, but as I will discuss later, our brains have mirror neurons. These are the nerve cells that cause us to be able to vicariously experience what we are reading, viewing on television, eye witnessing, and so forth.

By doing this, the reader is accumulating a small amount of negative karma that will negatively affect them in this or their future lives. This is just at a subtle level. On a larger scale, some readers will identify with characters in such novels and actually become motivated to do some of the things of which they have read. Then they will be gaining a lot of negative karma, both from their motivation and their sexual acts.

Therefore, with your precious time and life, why not read about the opposite – harmonious, mutually fulfilling love-making in committed relationships? Then you will exercise your mirror neurons in the opposite way, and positive karma and happiness will be the result. And you may even identify with some of the characters and enact their behavior in your own life – and won't your intimate partner be happy about that! Through making them happy, more positive karma will be produced, which will lead to even more happiness for you and your partner now and in the future.

Instead of reading about killing and theft – more trashy fiction – read, for example, the autobiography of Albert Schweitzer, the famed humanitarian and doctor who did everything in his power to save lives and give to those in need.

Senseless Chatter

Unfortunately once again, Westerners spend a lot of time engaging in "senseless chatter". What Tibetan Buddhists mean by this is speech that is unwholesome, divisive, gossipy, and in any way harmful to yourself or others. Similar to filling most of our reading time with trashy fiction, too much of our speech is subtly harmful to others. So when you are gossiping about what the neighbors are doing, or whom the mayor or president is screwing, this is activating our mirror neurons to create negative karma.

Stop squandering your opportunity to make progress toward enlightenment through the spoken word! Instead, talk about things that are going to be beneficial to others, and not just fill the air with sound. Sometimes it's okay to just remain silent. While your colleagues may be laughing with you as you ridicule the company president, they may actually wonder if you are doing the same thing about them when they are not present. And in subtle ways like these, a culture bordering on paranoia can evolve in the workplace or at home, making things uncomfortable and unhappy for everyone.

In the work environment, for example, you could simply listen with empathy to someone who is experiencing job stress that day. In this way, you will ease their stress a bit, and you will experience happiness yourself from having been of help. At the dinner table, instead of maliciously gossiping about the neighbors you could talk about ways in which your family could benefit them, or your community. By doing so, instead of creating a cycle of unhappiness and negative karma, through positive speech you will be nurturing the causes of happiness for yourself and your neighbors.

Indulging in Addictions

A huge part of what we do in the West falls under the category of indulging in addictions. This leads us away from unconditional serenity, which was discussed at length in Chapter Five. This addictive behavior also leads us to waste much of our time in our precious human life. Think of all of the time that you spend trying to acquire material things, such as that new BMW. And add to that the time that you spend seeking sensual pleasures, such as dinner with the latest person that you're dating at the finest restaurant in town. Further, add to this the time that you spend chasing after approval and status – like the fact that you are not satisfied with the publishing company with which you are currently linked, and your "need" to have your books published by an even more prestigious company. Add to all these the time that you spend seeking out happiness for its own sake, and struggling like hell to avoid the least bit of unhappiness, even for the sake of reaching a long-term goal.

∽

I don't mean to be completely condemning of all these things. In fact, if you do condemn them, this can increase their grip. However, to use your precious human life well, simply reduce their hold on you. If you don't, you could spend almost all of your time engaging in senseless chatter, writing trashy fiction, and indulging in addictions. So, to loosen their hold while still enjoying them some of the time, stick with a rational preference such as, "I can enjoy approval, sensual pleasure, getting new houses or cars, and I can certainly enjoy being happy! But I don't absolutely need these things, and stubbornly refuse to spend all of my time chasing after them. Then, I can devote a lot of my time to living and writing, and actualizing this precious opportunity which is my life."

In the discussion above, I have shown how we use our time unproductively. But that still doesn't answer the question, "Why do we do this?" I think that there are mainly two reasons. The first deals with the lack of mindfulness or awareness of how we use our time. In other words, we're not even aware of how we use our time, so it's not so surprising that we don't use it very well. We don't put a lot of thought into how to prioritize our time. This is more of a Zen Buddhist concept, in which the solution is to become mindful and aware.

A Tibetan Buddhist approach relating to our poor use of time is the concept of emptiness. We don't often think about the fact that everything is selfless, empty, and impermanent, and that it's not going to be there forever. So, most of the time, we unconsciously assume that we going to be alive in this life forever, and thus we don't feel a sense of urgency of making the most of our lives in the here and now. With this unconscious assumption, we think that we can put off starting to use our life well until tomorrow, next week, next month, or even next year!

Before we know it, practically our whole life has gone by and we haven't done much to take advantage of it. By doing *Assignment 7.1*, in a thorough way, you can begin to do just the opposite of this, which is to use your precious human life well! You will do this by learning about what I call the "three wisdoms", and then putting your knowledge about these into practice.

Assignment 7.1
Developing the Three Forms of Wisdom

Develop a strong determination to personally possess what I call the "three wisdoms".

1. The Wisdom of Auspiciousness

The first is wisdom concerning the very positive situation in which you currently exist. I call this the "wisdom of auspiciousness". Why not really, really be aware of this all the time? Remind yourself daily that you have obtained the precious human embodiment. From a Tibetan Buddhist perspective, it may have taken eons for this to happen. It is a result of having practiced perfect morality in your past lives. Now you have this human life, with all its freedoms. Constantly remind yourself of having these and therefore putting effort into studying Dharma books or the key texts of your spiritual tradition, and put these new understandings into practice. If it helps you, develop at the end of each day a list of the small things that you have done to actualize your Buddha nature on a Buddha Dharma Performance Form (*Worksheet 10. 1*), or invent a similar self-reinforcement program on your own.

In addition to keeping this record, go ahead and write all of the things that make you and your life circumstances incredibly favorable within your spiritual tradition on *Worksheet 7.1: Wisdom of Auspiciousness*. Some of the more general ones have been noted in this chapter, such as having obtained the precious human form, meeting with the teachings of your tradition, and having the opportunity to practice them. But there are certainly some things that are unique about your own individual situation, so be sure to note these. For example, you may have inherited a million dollars from your parents, which gives you an incredible opportunity to practice the generosity transcendence with some of the interest and earnings of your assets, as well as being able to practice almost full-time as a result of your inheritance. Or you may be very young, perhaps even a teenager, and you would want to put this on your *Wisdom of Auspiciousness Form*, located at the end of this chapter. Not only have you obtained this precious human life, with all its liberties and opportunities, but you have also discovered the transcendent wisdom of your spiritual tradition at a young age, thus having many years in which to actualize the potential that lies within the teachings of your tradition in your life.

Go over what you have written on this form on a daily basis, slowly and meditatively, for at least 30 days. Then, any time you feel yourself slipping back into lethargy and lack of vigilance about living your life in a robust spiritual manner, review what you have already written on *Worksheet 7.1* and add further items which have, since then, come to your awareness.

2. The Wisdom of Mindfulness

This is the one that is most popular in the West, although I think that actually practicing it is not so popular. What I am talking about here is simple awareness – and particularly, awareness of your time and your life and how you are using them. This is the first step to using them better. For example, you can gain awareness of how much time you are spending writing through regular use of the *Writing Time Log form* (*Worksheet 8.3*), explained in Chapter Eight. But you could develop a similar form for anything that's important to you. You could develop one to log the amount of time that you spend doing altruistic activities, being with your family, developing your professional life more fully, and so forth.

There is also mindfulness of what you're doing in the present moment. The delightful Zen Buddhist monk, Thich Nhat Hanh, for instance, describes these in great detail. One part of your assignment is to read some of his books, especially *The Miracle of Mindfulness*, and his audio programs, such as *The Present Moment*. He describes being mindful while brushing your teeth, for instance. In other words, while you are brushing your teeth, really appreciate and enjoy the fact that you are able to be alive and brushing your teeth. He even says, "There can be a lot of enjoyment in teeth brushing!" And indeed there can be tremendous enjoyment in really appreciating that you are alive, brushing your teeth, and having the time and resources to do so, and that you still have your teeth! He talks about how to be really mindful and aware while washing the dishes, and how this can be a very pleasurable activity, provided that you're really "there" and not thinking about something stressful.

So you can be mindful during any activity, and I'm particularly recommending that you be mindful of what you're doing with your life. You can take an inventory in this regard every evening, or midway through the day and in the evening. During these times, reflect on how you have lived during the day – or half day – and see if you are really living in accord with your most strongly felt values.

Often, on retreats – even secular ones – people are asked to reflect on how they are living their lives, and if they are really living in the way that they truly desire. By doing this assignment regularly, you will be bringing this important retreat component into every day, so that a year doesn't have to go by before you recognize that you'd like to make an adjustment in how you are spending your time.

3. Wisdom of Wisdom

This is the most important wisdom, to which the esteemed writer, translator and professor Robert Thurman gives the eloquent name the "wisdom transcendence". It is actually one – the most important – of what Tibetan Buddhists call the "six perfections". The other five are generosity, enthusiasm, concentration, morality, and patience. Wisdom is considered to be the most important perfection because once you have it, it's relatively easy to have all of the other five as well.

The "wisdom of wisdom" is your most powerful weapon against wasting your precious human existence. This is the wisdom that understands and even "sees" emptiness. Because things are empty of an intrinsic or core existence, they're impermanent. Another way of saying it is that their present form will pass away, just like your present form – human embodiment – will pass away. (Stick with me as I explain the concept of emptiness. It seems tricky at first, but even this trickiness is empty, like an illusion, and before you know it, you'll grasp this concept like knowing your name.) With an understanding of emptiness, you will use your precious life well and make the most of it in terms of your writing and living.

"But what the heck is emptiness?" you're probably still thinking. Well, I'm going to give you three meditations that are going to help you to really get your mind around this idea. You can log your time spent meditating on *Worksheet 7.2: Meditation Time Log*. This is virtually identical to the *Writing Time Log* (*Worksheet 8.3*), except on this form, you are going to "log" the time that you spend meditating on the "three wisdoms", or doing any of the other meditations that have been assigned.

Please don't let all of the forms and worksheets in this book overwhelm you a bit, because I only ask that you try them and then use them to the extent that they are useful to you.

Meditations on the "Three Wisdoms"

Here we go with the first meditation on the "wisdom of wisdom", or emptiness. For superb instruction on meditation posture, and so forth, see Philip Kapleau's marvelous book, *The Three Pillars of Zen*.

> You are to sit on a cushion in your meditation space, with your legs gently crossed and your hands on your thighs. If you have trouble sitting on a cushion, by all means sit in an upright position in a chair with both hands on your

thighs. Breathe in deeply through your nose, as if the air were going into your stomach, and then exhale slowly out of your mouth.

Clear your mind of all ordinary concerns and have a positive motivation, which is to evolve yourself and, through this, have a greater capacity for freedom and enjoyment, as well as the ability to help others. Then, simply allow an image of a crystal clear lake at nighttime to come into your mind. Really, really allow this image to emerge with as much detail as possible.

See the moon reflected in this clear lake. See the image of the moon change a bit due to small ripples in the water, and even a fish jumping out of the water here and there. Maintain this visualization for 5–20 minutes, depending on your tolerance and how much you are enjoying it. My idea is that this can be really enjoyable, and always be sure to stop a little bit before you feel completely ready to stop, which will make you eager to return to meditating.

In this meditation, observe how the image changes as a cloud moves in front of the moon, during which time the reflection in the water totally changes. Realize in your meditation that the image of the moon in the lake won't even be there when the sun is out the next day. This is emptiness!

The image of the moon at night in the clear lake was completely empty of permanent existence. You will see this beyond a shadow of a doubt in your meditation. Realize in your meditation that everything – yes, everything! – is like that image of the moon at night on the pristine lake. Nothing is exempt from emptiness! The book from which you are reading these words, your physical body, everything around you – including the people around you – are all empty of permanent existence. So rejoice in them, and rejoice in yourself, because you and they exist in this form now and can appreciate one another, but this won't always be the case. So, take advantage of it while it is! Most importantly, appreciate the opportunity that is in front of you to achieve enlightenment, salvation, or whatever name your particular tradition gives to the highest point to which a human being can evolve spiritually. And record the time on your *Meditation Time Log* during which you spend meditating – toward that ultimate end!

Now for the second meditation to further increase your ability to experientially understand the "wisdom of wisdom", and thereby make the most of your marvelous human life.

Get into your meditation posture, in the space in which you typically meditate, just as in the first meditation. Clear your mind of all mundane concerns, and breathe slowly in through your nose and out through your mouth. Remind yourself to have the ultimate, positive motivation of wanting to reach the highest state of spiritual evolution of which you are capable, in order to be able to most skillfully help sensitive beings. This time, allow the image of a huge oak tree to come into your mind. Really, really visualize it in every detail, while continuing to breathe slowly in through your nose and out through your mouth.

Release any resistance you have to feeling buoyant and blissful! Imagine the tree in the summer, with squirrels scurrying here and there to discover acorns. Then allow yourself to imagine the tree approach autumn, when all the leaves turn brown and fall to the ground, imagine the squirrels still chasing the acorns, and scurrying into their holes in the tree with their newfound treasures. Then imagine the passage of the tree into winter.

Imagine this happening over and over again until the tree becomes too old or damaged to sustain itself. Then, as if you were in the time machine depicted in that magnificent book by H G Wells, you can see the branches falling to the ground and ultimately the entire tree falling to the ground.

Then see there finally being nothing that even slightly resembles an oak tree, and perhaps see grass and flowers beginning to grow in its place. This once again illustrates emptiness!

The oak tree, which originally seems so solid and stable, was actually not solid at all. And once again, everything is of the same nature as the oak tree or the image of the moon on the lake at night. Both are like an Illusion, in that their existence is temporary. The awareness that nothing is immune to emptiness can motivate you to really use your life well, since you are empty of permanence and won't always be around – at least not in your present form. So make the best use of your days and hours – starting now! – to push yourself to achieve the highest level of spiritual evolution of which you are capable, which in the Tibetan Buddhist tradition is becoming a fully enlightened being.

Having completed these meditations on inanimate objects, you're now ready to fully realize your own emptiness in this third meditation. In the traditional Tibetan Buddhist meditation, you meditate on how each of the elements of which you are made is empty. The following meditation that I develop is a bit more concrete, and has an appeal to Westerners because of our familiarity with quantum physics.

Again, assume the meditation posture in your ideal meditation place, and become prepared to meditate between 5–20 minutes, depending on your tolerance, and remembering to stop a bit before you feel like stopping.

Once you feel that you are in the meditation mode, imagine a replica of yourself sitting in front of you, as if you were looking into a mirror. Then, imagine that the mirror becomes kind of funky and you are now seeing a different image of yourself, because you are seeing the tiny quantum particles of which you are made.

Then, allow yourself to see only quantum particles, in the form of a person, moving at mind-blowing speeds. But let yourself see big amounts of empty space between the particles, to be consistent with the reality that you are made mostly of empty space – how much more of a depiction of emptiness can you get?

Really get a taste of experiencing yourself in this manner. You are not solid or permanent at all, but made of tiny particles moving at incredible speeds, within space that is mostly empty. This ultimately takes the form of living tissue, which is extremely pliable and impermanent. Look at your legs, arms, stomach, chest, face, and every part of your body and really develop awareness of the fact that you are a wonderful, living organism, but that no part of you is "solid" or permanent.

I'm not asking you to do this to belittle yourself, and in fact I want you to do just the opposite. I want you to realize how amazing you are, and all of the amazing things that you can do with yourself and your life, and what an impact you can have on the lives of others! And I don't want you to squander this opportunity by believing that you are permanent, like a sculpture that will last forever. Because by realizing your emptiness, you will feel a strong drive to both appreciate yourself and utilize your life in the best manner possible, through developing your subtle inner enlightenment nature, and benefiting other beings. Your awareness of emptiness can allow you to celebrate your own life and that of others, realize how amazing it is, and in no way whatsoever to belittle it.

Another implication of your growing awareness of your "wisdom of wisdom" is that everything is possible. If everything that exists didn't exist in the nature of emptiness (if there were no "wisdom of wisdom") then what you see is what you get. Everything would remain the way that it is, and that would be that! So there wouldn't be any reason to try to change anything, including yourself. But since everything is empty and therefore infinity changeable, there is nothing at all that is immune to being changed!

If you are now suffering, there can be an end to your suffering. If you have not yet been of much service to others, you can become of almost infinite benefit to others. If you are at present unenlightened, you can become enlightened. If you have not yet published your first book, this is empty of inherent existence, which is to say that you can have your first book published. The same line of reasoning applies to more worldly concerns. If you haven't yet reached the level that you'd like to reach financially, because of emptiness there is room for optimism about being able to slowly but dramatically change your financial status. If you are single, this is completely empty of permanence, and you can discover a loving relationship with another person.

You can meditate on any of these things in the same manner in which I guided you through the three meditations above. For example, if you don't presently have your first book on the market, you can at first visualize the details of your present state, see those details dissolving into emptiness, and then see an alternate reality emerging in which your book is on the market, and you can visualize each of the intermediate steps. Know that in the truth of emptiness there is the promise of possibilities for your evolution that are without limit!

Worksheet 7.1:
Wisdom of Auspiciousness

"You have already attained a situation which is very favorable. You have obtained your precious human life and you have met with the teachings."

His Holiness Ling Rinpoche

What about your life is most favorable, or auspicious for writing and living the principles of your spiritual path? Put a brief summary of the most important favorable conditions below, thinking of conditions that apply to all people as well as ones unique to yourself.

1.
2.
3.
4.
5.
6.
7.
8.

Worksheet 7.2:
Meditation Time Log

Meditation Time Log for: _____

Time	Comments
6:00	
6:30	
7:00	
7:30	
8:00	
8:30	
9:00	
9:30	
10:00	
10:30	
11:00	
11:30	
12:00	
12:30	
1:00	
1:30	
2:00	
2:30	
3:00	
3:30	
4:00	
4:30	
5:00	
5:30	
6:00	
6:30	
7:00	
7:30	
8:00	
8:30	
9:00	
9:30	
10:00	
10:30	
11:00	
11:30	
12:00	
12:30	

Chapter Eight

SOURCES OF TRANSCENDENT WISDOM FOR LIVING AND WRITING

The sources of supreme wisdom for your writing and your life have been incidentally presented in previous chapters. This chapter is going to be devoted to the topic specifically, with more depth and detail.

The issue of the importance of your mentor, for your progression on the path to enlightenment, will be discussed later in this chapter. However, it is worth pointing out that guidance by a guru to fulfill your supreme purpose is not necessarily due to the guru's being the *source* of supreme knowledge, realization, and wisdom.

The word "wisdom" here is not exclusively meant in the sense of seeing the lack of inherent existence in phenomena. The wisdom that sees emptiness is *part* of it, but what is being discussed in this chapter is wisdom being any knowledge or realizations that benefit you and help you to benefit others – from a Dharma perspective – which can then be shared with others through your writing. You can share your realizations, and you can also share your unique way of expressing them with others.

You may have received teachings on the "six perfections" a dozen times and read ten books that discuss them, but when you hear them expressed in a *different* way, you may be able to finally understand them. And you may be a person uniquely predisposed through karma to deliver a particular type of wisdom to particular people. Of course, if you are fully enlightened, which you are not, you could adjust your writing to fit the needs and level of understanding of any reader.

Eight Sources of Transcendent Wisdom

The specific sources of wisdom for your writing and your life, given a proper Mahayana motivation, are enumerated below:

1. Reading Supremely Inspired Texts

One important source that is often underemphasized is reading. Not just any reading, but the reading of the work of supremely accomplished practitioners such as the works of His Holiness the Fourteenth Dalai Lama, Lama Zopa Rinpoche, Lama Thubten Yeshe, Lama Tsongkhapa, Trungpa Rinpoche, Sogyal Rinpoche, Pabongka Rinpoche and others; also the autobiographies of these spiritual masters and biographies written by qualified individuals. This would include, for example, *Dalai Lama*, the recently released authorized biography of His Holiness. It needs to be emphasized that for this to be of supreme benefit, bodhimind needs to be the aspiration. Other works include *My Land and My People* and *Freedom in Exile*, also both by His Holiness.

Reading books like these is the very opposite of reading trashy fiction, which leaves negative imprints on your consciousness and generates negative karma. When you are reading one of these spiritual biographies or autobiographies, your mirror neurons equip you to vicariously experience what you are reading. This will generate positive karma. In fact, this is spiritual practice. You could take refuge and generate bodhimind at the beginning of your reading and dedicate the merit that is accumulated at the end of your reading experience – dedicate it to the perfect, complete enlightenment for the benefit of all living beings, without exception. You can derive incredible benefit from such sources.

An individual can happen upon such a book anywhere – in prison, for instance; the person will read it, take it to heart, and allow it to influence his or her consciousness.

A profound life transformation can then take place, indeed. You have certainly heard stories such as this. The Venerable Thubten Chodron, the Tibetan Buddhist nun and author of many helpful books, first encountered Dharma by observing an announcement of a Dharma talk. In writing about this author and practitioner, I am reminded that I had received a number of teachings concerning Tara[9] practice. But almost nothing clicked until I read her book, *How to Free Your Mind: Tara the Liberator*, and now Tara practice helps me greatly.

Similarly, I read a book by His Holiness about Mentor Devotion before attending an 11-day retreat in which Gehlek Rinpoche taught this practice. Because my mind had been primed from reading, when I attended the teaching it was as if I had experienced it previously, and Lama Chopa is now one of my daily practices. I am in no way suggesting that Dharma books are a *substitute* for being linked with a qualified guru. But they can be a supplement to your connection to your guru. The place to begin your reading will often be transcripts of your guru's teachings.

2. Searching for Underlying Principles

Many people experience difficulty in reading texts, especially if they are of a complex or technical nature. You may lose the entire train of thought in a text through being distracted by an unusual word. But you don't need to be distracted in this way. The modern-day philosopher, Mortimer J Adler, gives powerful advice to the reader in his work, *How to Read a Book: the Classic Guide to Intelligent Reading*. One of the many pieces of advice Adler gives about reading complex or pre-modern texts is to not get hung up on the obscure word, but instead to read for *underlying principles*. For example, you can read a book such as Isaac Newton's *Principia* and, although it contains a lot of mathematics, you can understand it without much knowledge of mathematics if you read for underlying principles.

Even with a Mahayana motivation, you may avoid seemingly esoteric Dharma books if you don't use this method. Upon re-reading or receiving teachings, aspects that at first eluded you will become completely illuminated. Furthermore, this reading will prime you to understand Dharma teachings that would have otherwise been somewhat obscure. Do not, however, read material for which a specific initiation is required unless you have received the appropriate initiation.

3. Dharma Essence of Non-Dharma Books

There are also non-Dharma books that can be of benefit. For example, in Alfred Adler's book, *Social Interest: A Challenge to Mankind*, Dr Adler noticed that whenever he could convince his psychotherapy patients to perform altruistic activities, they invariably lost many of the symptoms which initially brought them into treatment. Some patients went further and became energetic, creative, and productive people though developing social interest, which is a bit analogous to what we in the Mahayana tradition would call other-cherishing. I write "a bit analogous" because other-cherishing goes beyond mundane social interest – it includes bodhimind, renunciation of the eight worldly addictions, and so forth. It is nevertheless apparent that Dr Adler was on a similar track with the Mahayana Buddhists in his discovery that through benefiting others, you are benefited as well.

This is similar to Bill Wilson's seminal insight, which led to the founding of Alcoholics Anonymous. Mr Wilson discovered that the *only* way he could remain sober was to work with other alcoholics to help them achieve and maintain sobriety. He furthermore realized that he couldn't create all of the causes and conditions himself – there had to be receptivity to the "teachings" of Alcoholics Anonymous. Victor E Frankel admitted that one of the ways in which he had been able to keep himself alive during years in concentration camps was through helping others. In his writings, Dr Frankel revealed that many times he felt as though he was benefiting more than the prisoners he was treating.

Frankel was a medical doctor known for creating a makeshift clinic and treating the sick in the concentration camp where he was imprisoned, as well as for providing help and advice to the camp guards who, in the eyes of the impoverished prisoners, clearly lived in the lap of luxury. Following his release, he returned to his psychiatric practice with greatly increased effectiveness. Much as Dr Adler observed, Frankel found that many of his patients were helped dramatically when he convinced them to become involved in volunteer work or other altruistic pursuits. He taught in a medical school in Vienna and instructed his medical students and psychiatric interns not to aim for worldly success, but to aim at making a substantial contribution to humanity.

Paradoxically, these students and residents often went on to achieve worldly success simply as a by-product of the beneficial contributions they made. They often were quite indifferent to the gains and achievements and became highly philanthropic. Dr Frankel bears his insights in his books, particularly *Man's Search for Meaning* and *The Doctor and the Soul*. In his keynote address at The Evolution of Psychotherapy conference in 1995, he said that out of all his books (more than 30 published) these two were the only ones that became well known, yet they were the two in which he had the least concern for professional advancement. He even considered publishing *Man's Search for Meaning* anonymously, but was convinced not to do this by his publisher who said that an anonymous title would not reach as many people who could benefit from it.

While these are obviously not books written within the Buddhist traditions, certain parallels can be drawn. These resources, and the wisdom contained in them may even help to make spiritual progress for those who are not predisposed, through karma, to derive benefit from Dharma readings and teachings per se. Hence recommending and teaching such books could help such persons in their development and overcoming of obstacles.

4. Mentor Devotion

There is no greater source of wisdom, inspiration and so forth than your mentor or guru. The most important thing for you to do is to find an appropriate spiritual master, if you have not already done so. There is a process whereby you critically look at the qualities of a perspective spiritual master in the beginning, but then you "place yourself completely under his care," to quote from His Holiness Ling Rinpoche's transcript of the Song of the Four Mindfulnesses. His Holiness Ling Rinpoche was the Senior Tutor of His Holiness the Fourteenth Dalai Lama. From your mentor you take refuge in the Three Jewels[10], receive Dharma teachings, master the lam-rim[11], and receive Highest Yoga Tantra (Vajrayana)[12] and other initiations.

You also receive direct transmissions of oral teachings – this you cannot get from a book; regardless of the quality of the discourse contained therein. With initiations come vows and practice commitments. With the proper mentor-disciple relationship and connection, enlightenment can be created as if by hand, to paraphrase His Holiness' transcript. If you are not yet an advanced practitioner who has obtained realizations, your connection with a living master is essential. Mahayana Buddhism is a living tradition, and it is through your spiritual master that you receive this living tradition. Your amount of receptiveness can be increased through the suggestions in the section above entitled Searching for Underlying Principles. Yet there is no substitute for the spiritual master's guidance in transcending samsara's suffering and nirvana's complacency. In the same sense that a ceramicist is essential for producing a piece of ceramic fine art, without his or her guidance you might wind up firing yourself to death in the kiln instead of having pottery fire in the kiln! In living and writing, there is no greater source of inspiration or fire than your spiritual master.

5. Receiving Teachings

After years of receiving teachings, studying transcripts and other Dharma books, doing concentrated and analytical meditation, mastering the lam-rim, beginning to master Highest Yoga Tantra practices – after having received appropriate initiations – all under the direction of your qualified spiritual master, and in engaging in *dialogue* with other senior sanga members, you may be ready and have the inclination to *write*. In writing there can be discovery and opportunity to make contributions that will benefit others on the path, and you may indeed be uniquely qualified to make certain specific contributions. For example, I make unique contributions due to having a background in cognitive behavioral therapy, and I have the ability and inclination to link this with Dharma material in such a way as to help a reader to live and write creatively. *Write for Your Lives* represents such a synthesis, yet further insights from the behavioral sciences may be brought in to show how they complement and supplement the sutra-level aim of lam-rim to eliminate your afflictive emotions.

A concept from Mortimer J Adler comes to mind. Adler has written that books can be analogous to absent teachers. This is also one of the reasons why Dharma books are to be respected very highly; we are not to walk on them, jump over them, set mundane books or other objects on top of them, and so forth. Again, given proper qualification, why should you not write of decreasing the ten non-virtuous actions and increasing the ten positive ones? What is being repeated is that you may be *uniquely* qualified to write about them or at least about certain aspects of them. And given that you are writing based on the highest of altruistic aspirations, you may be able to make very important contributions.

For example, simply the clarity and elegant simplicity of your writing style is a way of being uniquely qualified – this is, of course, assuming you are qualified in the supreme sense and not just in your mundane writing ability. I, for instance, know from research in the behavioral sciences that for most individuals it is more effective to construct positive actions than to simply diminish the negative ones. This may not, however, have been part of the worldview at the time when the original sutras were written. Hundreds of studies have shown that people can gradually build positive behavior, and even thoughts and emotions, through sequential approximations.

Furthermore, learning new actions is best done with rewards rather than via punishment. You can receive these rewards from others, give them to yourself, or both. This also seems to go along with the spirit of self-compassion and other-cherishing, which underlies the Mahayana Buddhist perspective. Other strategies that emerge from contemporary behavioral science are the Five-Column Technique and Rational Emotive Imagery which I discuss in Chapter Four.

So again, after years of receiving teachings from your spiritual master, engaging in dialogue with senior sanga members and so forth, you may be inclined to write. Through your background and karma, you may be uniquely equipped to make specific, significant contributions that will be of great benefit to others, and through this process of integration – with bodhimind – your writing can become a source of transcendent wisdom.

6. Enlightenment-Oriented Motivation

In real estate, there is a common saying, "location, location, location". In other words, the location of a home, business or piece of property is of pivotal importance. Concerning the practice of writing, we could say, "motivation, motivation, motivation". Even if you are writing already but still have a self-cherishing motivation, your writing will not be Dharma practice.

With this motivation, you can develop what I call "the lifeline of books" concept. Mortimer J Adler developed a list called Great Books of the Western world. If you examine these books, you will find that most of them begin with extensive outlines. For example, if you read Aristotle's *Ethics*, you will see that the outline is five or ten pages long, depending upon the translation – it is extremely detailed. As a creative individual, you will generate more ideas for writing beneficial books than you could have time to even begin in this lifetime; yet, you may have just enough time to write their outlines. Therefore, when you leave this life, in addition to leaving behind your body, possessions, friends, family, and everything else, you can also leave your own lifeline of books. These are the outlines for the beneficial books that you *did not* have time to write in this lifetime, so that others can put their minds to work on the creation of these books.

This is especially true for people who, when given a sound idea, find it relatively easy to transform the concept into a book, even though they could not have developed the concept on their own. This outline does not leave a legacy in a worldly sense but is used to help transform our world in a favorable direction. Do not be attached to this outline at the time of your death or at any other time. Instead, have it be truly based on cherishing others and renunciation of the eight worldly concerns – see that it contains outlines for manuscripts and teachings that will help to guide others to the city of liberation. Your continuation or continuations may make use of your lifeline of books in future lives.

7. Realizations from Analytical Meditation and Dreams

Of course, there are realizations from analytical and concentrated meditation and from dreams. These are also sources of transcendent wisdom for your living and writing. Engage in dialogue with senior persons in your sanga about your realizations. Depending upon the nature of your relationship with your spiritual master, you may discuss these with him or her as well. Poignant insights can come from dreams and during the Yoga of Sleeping if you have received appropriate initiations and teachings about doing this type of practice. You can write these in the morning or during the night if you awaken. Sleep and dreams are like bardo[13] experiences. Just as we forget in rebirth after the bardo of becoming, we also tend to quickly forget our dreams after we wake up. Thus, it can be important to make note of auspicious insights fast after awakening. However, it is crucial to include most of these insights in dialogue with your spiritual teachers and friends. Otherwise, your ideas can become idiosyncratic to the degree that they take you not only off the path of Dharma, but even away from wholesome worldly endeavors.

Dr Ernest L Rossi has recently had a book published called *The Breakout Heuristic*. In this book, he documents his and others' studies of the integrative processes that happen in the mind during sleep. Similarly, Herbert Benson, the world-renowned professor of medicine at Harvard Medical School, recently wrote a book called *The Breakout Principle*. He also documented the integrative brain activities that occur during sleep and rest, and the solutions to problems that are often born out of sleep, rest or even simple distraction. The studies reported by both of these authors support the notion of how sleep, rest, and distraction can end in creative solutions to problems.

I often find that when I am having difficulty with a practice, I go easy on myself. I complete the practice and then I sleep on it – literally, as the practice will often gain additional clarity only the next morning. A shower can even be a source of distraction during which or after which creative solutions to problems and fresh insights emerge.

8. Purification Practices

The last source of transcendent wisdom for living and writing which is going to be discussed here is purification. A number of Dharma practices involve purification to some extent, but there are others specifically intended for this purpose. Lama Tsongkhapa, for example, received teachings from Manjushri – the Buddha of Wisdom – after engaging in extensive and prolonged purification practices while on retreat, during which he was seeking to obtain teachings from Manjushri. His precious Song of the Four Mindfulnesses and Three Principal Aspects of the Path to Enlightenment exist now as a result of Lama Tsongkhapa's extensive and long purification practices pursued on this retreat.

In the Mahayana tradition, one of the most celebrated purification practices is Varjasattva Purification. If done at the Vajrayana level, it is necessary to first receive an initiation and teachings from a qualified master on this practice. A book you may want to consult which contains many sutra-level purification practices is Lama Zopa Rinpoche's *Ultimate Healing: The Power of Compassion*. Purification practices can help you make progress on the path to enlightenment for the benefit of all sentient beings. Your negative karma is mainly what is being purified since it creates obstructions on the path to enlightenment. Negative karma also results in disease processes, which can be helped or cured through purification practices. Through removing obstructions, these practices can also lead to transcendent wisdom for your living and writing.

Of course, we always want to dedicate the merit that has been accumulated during these practices to the benefit of all living beings, without exception.

Assignment 8.1:
Tapping into Transcendent Wisdom

You now know about the eight sources of transcendent wisdom for fully living Buddha Dharma and writing. This is an exercise about accessing some of these sources. So, let's try tapping into three of the sources simultaneously – as you will see, the methods for tapping into the sources overlap. But for now, let's try tapping into Reading Supremely Inspired Texts, an example of which would be the book of a great master, either living or from the past. This book definitely does not qualify! Your assignment is simply to read for an hour or so immediately before going to sleep for the night. Then you are going to plug your reading into another source of transcendent wisdom, which are Realizations from Analytical Meditation and Dreams. It wouldn't even be a bad idea to keep the book in the room with you while you're sleeping to remind yourself of what you have read were you to awaken. But even if you don't wake up at all during the night, your brain is going to work on the material, digesting and integrating it, while you are sleeping. The esteemed pediatrician, Martin Levine, M.D., extensively discusses the brain's potential to review material that was learned immediately before going to sleep, at least four times after falling asleep.

Do this with an enlightenment-oriented motivation – for the benefit of all living being – and now you are using a third source of wisdom, Enlightenment-Oriented Motivation. Adding this third element to your process will increase the flavor and strength of the wisdom that you acquire through reading.

Of course, you can choose from any number of books, for example Pabongka Rinpoche's classic, *Liberation in the Palm of Your Hand,* or a more recent book such as *Wisdom Energy: Basic Buddhist Teachings,* by Lama Yeshe and Lama Zopa Rinpoche[14]. Or why not any one of the books written by Chogyam Trungpa Rinpoche[15]? To a certain extent, you're going to have to use your own judgment to determine which books are and which are not supremely inspired. And by saying, "supremely inspired" we are saying that the teachings within the book are emanations of an enlightened mind. However, to start with, please see my Suggested Reading list at the back of this book.

You can certainly use this method if you are a practitioner outside of the Buddhist tradition. A person of the Catholic faith, for example, might insert a book such as Saint Augustine's *City of God* into the formula outlined in this assignment. A person of the Jewish tradition might use one of the great classic works of Moses Maimonides, or a more modern book by an author such as Abraham Joshua Heschel or Elie Wiesel. If you are a Taoist, you might simply use some verses from the *Tao Te Ching*. If Sufi, why not start with one of the poems of Rumi – can you think of a better place at which to begin this journey?

Then, upon awakening, write the thoughts that are on your mind pertaining to what you read before going to sleep. Whatever they are, put them on paper. At this time, don't make discriminating judgments about which ideas are important, and which are not. Simply get them down, as close to the time that you awaken as possible. For your convenience and inspiration, please see *Worksheet 8.1: Upon Awakening*. Upon awakening from sleep, you are going to notice that new insights have awakened within you. Even if they don't at first seem directly related to the reading that you did before going to sleep, get your insights down on an Upon Awakening form as quickly as possible. Before using the form on the next page, be sure to make plenty of photocopies of it! Of course, this is because this is not a one time assignment – your journey of awakening the writer within is an ongoing process, which can not only continue throughout this lifetime – why not have it extend into future lifetimes? Why not *write for your lives*?

Worksheet 8.1:
Upon Awakening

Inspired Thoughts:

1.

2.

3.

4.

5.

6.

7.

8.

Assignment 8.2:
From Morning Notes to Manuscript

You have begun to get your insights onto paper through *Assignment 8.1*, having recorded them on *Worksheet 8.1: Upon Awakening*. This assignment is about further developing your ideas, and preparing them to be brought to your audience in the form of an article, book, poem, or story. It is key to understand that your *Upon Awakening* form, and the morning notes that you make on it are some of the raw material for your manuscript. I have written "some" because you are going to also be making notes to yourself at other times. For example, you may be in a business meeting when an insight comes to you. Whether in the morning or at the business meeting, jot the idea down in a notebook! This is an excellent tool because you can take it with you everywhere, and you won't look out of place writing in it, even during a formal business meeting.

For instance, during a recent business meeting, I actually had an interesting writing idea, which I jotted down in my Day Timer. The notes that I wrote down pertain to how I was keeping myself focused and calm during the meeting through a certain Dharma insight – *lo-jung* in particular. *Lo-jung* simply means "mind training", which can lead to a completely different way of looking at something which initially might seem disturbing. The manuscript I would create based on these ideas would be called something like, *The Buddha in the Board Room: Using Buddha Dharma to Transform Your Official and Everyday Business*. Obviously the readership for this would be broad and would go beyond hardcore organizational business, because as the subtitle implies, even everyday interactions are a kind of business, as well as an opportunity to practice. So these are the ways in which you get the ideas for your manuscript on paper, at least initially.

You will often find that the ideas that you have been jotting down over a period of time are actually the answer to a substantial intellectual or practical question. This brings us to *Worksheet 8.2: Explicit Questions, Large and Small*. This is your assignment. Think about the ideas that you have been jotting down over a period of time, or over just one day. What question do these ideas answer? For example, if you have been reading a book about traveling the path of the spiritual warrior, you may find that you have written down a lot of ideas about contemporary tools that can aid in this – tools that didn't exist when the book was written. So the question that your ideas answer may be something like "What contemporary tools can help people on the sacred path of the spiritual warrior most effectively?"

If you decide to write a manuscript, it will answer this question. Each chapter will answer a smaller, sub-question. Once you have answered all of your sub-questions, you will have written all of your chapters, and once you have written all your chapters, a draft of your manuscript is finished. This is a simple yet highly effective formula for producing a manuscript, with the ultimate aim of having it become a published book. Email me, have discussions with colleagues, or do the Five-Column Technique if you run into a snag during this process. The Five-Column Technique will often be of the greatest help because your difficulties will often result from thinking errors about the process in which you are engaged. This then leads to anxiety and other negative emotions, which hinder instead of helping your creative process. So, after you have been doing your Upon Awakening forms for a while, and writing other notes for yourself, then begin formulating questions and sub-questions, and do this on *Worksheet 8.2*, which is at the end of this chapter. As with other worksheets in this book, make plenty of photocopies before writing on the originals so that you can use them on an ongoing basis.

Worksheet 8.3: Writing Time Log Form is for the next phase of your work, after you have formulated your questions. Because, after you have written down your questions, the chapters aren't going to write themselves, are they? You need a tool to inspire your writing on a daily basis, or on however many days of a given week that you choose. Sometimes your writing won't even feel that inspired, especially at the beginning of a session, and you may need to just crunch out words for a while to get some momentum and inspiration going. This is where the *Writing Time Log Form* is of a lot of benefit. After your writing sessions, your assignment is to darken (color) in the time during which you have been writing.

Remember, during these writing sessions, any time you get off track, simply remind yourself of the question that you are answering through your writing. Focus on answering it in a way that is going to be of the greatest benefit to your reader. This motivation is pivotal, and not only applies to your writing, but to any kind of art or any creative endeavor. Never forget that even when you are not writing or doing art specifically, you are living, and the way that you live is the highest form of art. During your writing sessions, remembering to focus on being of the greatest benefit to your audience is very liberating because it automatically removes your ego (self-cherishing) from your writing or other artistic endeavor.

I recommend that you write on as many days of the week as your schedule permits, but try *not* to exceed two hours on any given day. If you do exceed this quota of time you will get some more words on paper, however the price will likely be a lot of fatigue, as well as what people in the behavioral school of psychology call "the post-reinforcement lag". This is a fancy way of saying that you will tend to skip your writing altogether the next day – or even the next *days* – and even if you don't skip them your writing will suffer in terms of quality. Also, by not disciplining yourself to stop writing after two hours in a given day, you will be increasing your risk for carpel tunnel syndrome, neck problems, and other physical afflictions.

It's better to have the consistent productivity that writing for up to two hours a day provides. Other rules of thumb are to try to write in the same place and at the same time of day. However, this

Worksheet 8.2: Explicit Questions, Large and Small

Large Question that your entire manuscript is going to answer or address, and which will guide all of your writing:

Sub-Questions/Chapters:

1.

2.

3.

4.

5.

6.

7.

8.

9.

10.

is certainly not always possible or even practical, yet it is preferable when you can work it out that way. Your body will get into a circadian rhythm where you are primed to be productive and creative in terms of the flow of your writing.

As has been mentioned previously, you'll want to tailor your writing environment to that which is optimally stimulating for you. For me, this is an aroma-filled coffee shop with a lot of activity going on around me. For you it may be a quiet study area, or somewhere in between these extremes.

The final rule of thumb is that you aren't to do many revisions before revision time! In other words, get the first draft of your book or article down on paper before you start doing any revisions. If you don't do this, you'll spend half of your writing time – or more! – doing revisions on an intermittent basis, when you don't even know that these revisions are useful because you don't have the objectivity of having a draft of your manuscript right in front of you, or at least a chapter. So, during these writing sessions, it's "damn the style manual and full speed ahead," so that you can maximize your productivity.

Worksheet 8.3 Writing Time Log Form

Time Log for: _____

Time	Comments
6:00	
6:30	
7:00	
7:30	
8:00	
8:30	
9:00	
9:30	
10:00	
10:30	
11:00	
11:30	
12:00	
12:30	
1:00	
1:30	
2:00	
2:30	
3:00	
3:30	
4:00	
4:30	
5:00	
5:30	
6:00	
6:30	
7:00	
7:30	
8:00	
8:30	
9:00	
9:30	
10:00	
10:30	
11:00	
11:30	
12:00	
12:30	

FROM MANUSCRIPT TO MARKET

Let's assume that you have been completing writing sessions as outlined in *Assignment 8.2* and now have a completed draft manuscript. This is a big assumption, but we can make it anyway! If you have not been writing, you can begin now. Unless you are a Shakespeare, you won't have a polished manuscript initially and so will need to improve it. When you do this, don't work for ten hours a day, even if you have that amount of time. You'll burn yourself out. Instead, plug the process of revising and polishing the manuscript into the same "maximum of two hours a day" plan that you used to write the manuscript to begin with.

Be sure to keep a positive mindset during these sessions, just as before when you were producing your draft. Keep in mind that you are working for the benefit of the reader, and even for the benefit of all sensitive beings. Whenever you get off track, remind yourself to have this motivation. And remember the question that you are answering through your writing or the answer that you are trying to make more accessible and pleasing to your readers through revising your manuscript.

When you have a fairly well-polished manuscript, now what do you do with it? How do you get it to your readers? If you are searching for a publisher or agent you need to start off with a solid book proposal. It is on the basis of this that an agent decides if they want to represent you, or a publisher decides if they are interested. Concerning some large, well-established publishing houses, they can only be approached through a literary agent.

In his excellent book, *How to Write a Book Proposal,* the literary agent and writer, Michael Larson, lists twelve good reasons why it is a good idea to complete your manuscript before your proposal. Once you've finished your manuscript, here are the ingredients for a complete book proposal:

- Pick as samples the two chapters that you feel are the best and have the greatest market appeal.
- Compile your manuscript's table of contents.
- Write a synopsis of your book ensuring it is a succinct summary of your manuscript and includes the distinctive contributions that your book has, as well as its major selling points.
- Make a promotion plan. This may not be requested by publishers, yet it is a key ingredient and can definitely make a difference in their acceptance or rejection of your proposal. The question that you have to answer in this section is, "How can this book be promoted to ensure its success, and in what ways can I help the publisher with this process?" When you are writing this section, markets (audiences) that you may not have previously considered will often appear in your mind. Also, you can't assume that the publisher or agent is going to spontaneously recognize the readership for your book.
- You may want to increase sales for your book by approaching top-notch experts who have name recognition to write a Foreword, Introduction, or Preface for your work. You may not intuitively connect

sales, money, and so forth to your book, yet you have to recognize that financial factors are part of the causes and conditions that will lead to its publication. The publication of your book is empty of inherent existence, so you need to nurture all of the causes and conditions that are going to make it happen initially, and subsequently sell well and remain in print.

- Finally, your proposal needs to include an author biography. This should include your past publications, if any, and everything about you and your background that is relevant to showing that you are qualified to write on the subject. Be positive and lively in this section, but do so without any exaggeration, because it will be immediately apparent to an experienced editor and you will lose credibility, not to mention the fact that you will have distorted the truth, which will have negative karmic consequences.

- At the very beginning of your proposal, include a table of contents for the proposal itself.

- On the cover page, list your name, address, phone numbers, email address, website (if you have one), the title of your book and sub-title, and a sentence beneath this that summarizes within 15 words your background and areas of expertise as they pertain to the book.

Where to submit your book proposal

First, there is a wonderful resource that is several volumes in length called, *The Literary Marketplace*. This is a periodical and should be in the reference section of your library. It includes, I believe, all of the major literary agents, publishing houses, and editors in the United States and Canada. At some university libraries, I have even found additional volumes, which include editors, agents, and publishers in other countries, including non-English speaking countries. So I recommend that you start here.

Alternatively, or in addition, you can go to your local bookstores and look at the books on subjects closely related to your own. Jot down the name of the publisher, as well as all contact information, including their website. There, you will usually find detailed information about what to send, and to whom. Publishers differ slightly in terms of what they require in book proposals, but generally they are very much along the lines of what I have described above. Remember to include a self-addressed envelope to encourage a response.

With cut-and-paste computer technology, once you have a solid proposal, you can easily tweak it to meet the submission requirements of any given publisher. *Worksheet 9.1: Book Proposal Completion Checklist* has been included at the end of this section to help you get through your first, or possibly next book proposal. Questions are included on the worksheet to prompt you regarding each section of the proposal. Ultimately, putting a check mark next to each question as that section is completed will help you feel a sense of exhilaration and inspiration as you proceed through the process of finalizing your proposal.

Getting a manuscript published is a competitive process, even with an excellent manuscript that will appeal to a large audience. You will probably need to submit it to a number of publishing houses, perhaps even dozens. To help you keep the faith during this process (your enlightenment-motivated orientation), I have developed *Worksheet 9.2: Book Proposal Submissions Record*. On this record, your assignment is to simply list the name of each publishing house or agent to which you submit your proposal, the date material was mailed, any follow-up to your initial submission, and comments regarding the follow-up. The simple process of recording this information is a way to help you maintain perspective during the lengthy and sometimes arduous process of taking the manuscript from book proposal to bookshelf.

Worksheet 9.1:
Book Proposal Completion Checklist

☐ Have I completed a title page, which includes the book's title and subtitle, my name, all pertinent contact information (website included, if applicable), with a statement beneath the subtitle that succinctly portrays my background and qualifications?

☐ Have I included a separate table of contents for the book proposal (remember, the editor or agent who examines the proposal will not necessarily want to read the sections in sequential order)?

☐ Have I completed and included a table of contents for the manuscript?

☐ Have I included a Foreword, Preface, or book cover quotes written by persons of stature with expertise directly related to the subject of the book?

☐ Have I included a section about the scope, precise length, and audience, keeping in mind that the editor or agent will be concerned with the size of the readership?

☐ Have I included a promotion plan that is realistic yet creative in the inclusion of the things I do to assist the publisher in effectively promoting my book (e.g., agreeing to give, or continue to give a specified number of workshops per month for one year following the book release date)?

☐ Have I included an author biography section, which realistically describes my expertise and background with regard to the subject of the book?

☐ Have I included one or more sample chapters, depending upon the requirements of the publisher or agent, which are not only informative and innovative, but also lively and engaging?

☐ Have I tailored my proposal to the precise specifications of the publisher or agent to whom it will be sent?

☐ Have I chosen an appropriate publisher or agent as my target?

Worksheet 9.2: Book Proposal Submissions Record

Date Sent	Publisher/Agent	Inclusions Sent	Response Received (Date if Applicable)	Date of Follow-up	Comments Regarding Follow-up

Many times, just using the *Book Proposal Submissions Record* will simply help you to not mentally exaggerate the number of proposals you have submitted. Otherwise, after submitting only 10 you may literally think and feel like you've submitted a 100! With this type of exaggeration in your mind, it's easy to lose heart and give up prior to finding a publisher for your manuscript. Perseverance, rejection practice, and learning to celebrate failure are the entire focus of the next section, so continue reading on!

Celebrating Failure and Rejection Practice

I bet that you didn't ever think that you would be asked to celebrate failure or practice rejection, or furthermore that there was anything to celebrate about failure! Why would you want to bother practicing rejection? Well, given that you have now completed your book proposal, and are beginning to send it to agents or publishers, it will be nothing short of a miracle if you don't have to deal with at least some level of rejection of your work. Some agents or publishers may not even send you a response. If it wasn't for this, I wouldn't have needed to put a column on the *Book Proposal Submissions Record* about following up if there is no response to your submission.

Some rejections will come in the form of standardized letters that agents simply send back to you in the return envelope you provided. Still others may be a bit more personalized, with the title of your book or manuscript inserted into the form letter – won't that make you feel special! The point is that you are going to have to deal with rejection, perhaps even a lot of it, and so you had best learn to practice rejection and celebrate failure on the path to succeeding as a bodhisattva author.

An acquaintance submitted her novel to 200 literary agents, and the first 199 rejected her work completely, without even a personalized rejection letter. The 200th agent liked the novel, and placed it with a top-notch publishing house. Even Albert Einstein had books rejected by publishers. In fact, in his legendary lack-of-common-sense fashion, he sent an original and only copy of a manuscript to a publisher, who did not publish or even return the original. It is thus lost to humanity forever; unless Albert Einstein's shrewder reincarnation makes an analogous contribution – and makes copies this time!

The Buddha Dharma Perspective

First, when you get rejection letters, instead of becoming immobilized by this, you can experience this rejection on behalf of living beings. In other words, see yourself experiencing this rejection or failure in place of other people – you are taking away their suffering. Therefore, you can be happy about this and rejoice. On the surface, this may seem ridiculous, until you remember that you are writing to benefit other sensitive beings, and why not benefit them, as above, during the process of bringing your work from book proposal to bookshelf?

Second, instead of seeing the rejection as undesirable, use your mind and imagination to recognize it as desirable. Think about the ways that it can be desirable for you and for your own situation. For me, rejections and failures concerning my writing have helped me to combat my ego and self-preoccupation, they have made me more resilient, and I have become much more prolific and much less of a perfectionist because I have realized that no matter how perfect my proposal may seem, some people are not going to like it. I have appreciated my ultimate successes more because of the rejections that came before them. But how will rejections benefit *you* – how will *you* look at them as desirable?

Third, from the perspective of Buddha Dharma, rejections can be seen as obstacles. As soon as you see them as not permanent and lacking inherent existence, then they cease to be an obstacle.

Fourth, and finally, you can know that your experience of obstacles, rejections, and failures results from negative karma that you have accumulated in the past. By going through these rejections, you can see this as purifying yourself of the negative karma, and even purifying others. You are experiencing the result of negative actions from the past, so you are getting these negative experiences out of the way. These rejections are probably a way of practicing empathy for others, and accumulating positive karma. In experiencing them, and persevering, you are going to be, by your example, encouraging others to take heart and persevere. And by persevering long enough to bring your manuscript from book proposal to bookshelf, the greater the difficulty, the more positive karma will have been accumulated.

The Cognitive Behavioral Therapy Perspective

After you have finished your book proposal, create a "Celebrating Failure" folder in which you will put evidence of all these rejections, whether they be in the form of rejection letters, e-mails, or a copy of the letters you sent that received no response at all. If you attend any of my workshops, you can see my very full "Celebrating Failure" folder, and hear some very juicy, as well as many very dry, excerpts! But the reason that you are accumulating this evidence of failure is to completely inoculate yourself to feelings of helplessness when you experience rejection.

What great actor or actress has not had to inoculate him- or herself to failure through innumerable auditions, especially at the beginning of a career? And with this immunization you will have given yourself a tremendous strength and treasure that you will be able to use throughout your career as a writer. The goal is to not be afraid of failure, and with this you will be optimally free and creative, won't you?

If you get depressed with receiving so many rejections, you can use the Buddha Dharma methods, above, to ease your pain. Actually, it is better to sit with the pain and fully inoculate yourself to the failure without any safety crutches. The same applies with regard to the Five-Column Technique from Chapter Four. You can ease your emotional pain by challenging the irrational cognitions which come into your mind when you receive rejections. But, better to sit with the uncertainty and discomfort, and fully inoculate yourself – experience what behavioral psychologists call "desensitization", where those nasty standardized rejection letters don't bother you a bit, and in fact propel you on to revise your proposal and send off still more!

Chapter Ten

HOW YOUR LIFE COULD BE, LIVING AND WRITING

What is going to be discussed in this chapter is clearly oriented to someone who wishes to live and write Buddha Dharma, especially in the Mahayana tradition. But keep in mind that even if you are following a different tradition, you can apply the basic structure presented in this chapter, while shifting the content to be consistent with your path. However, in whatever spiritual tradition you are following, there is going to be a basic sense about what is good and what is of value to pursue in your life.

In the Tibetan Buddhist, or Mahayana tradition, there is a clear sense about what to do with your life if you want to live it well and take full advantage of the opportunity that is your life. For instance, part of "the good" in the Tibetan tradition involves the three principal aspects of the path: letting go of conventional worldly concerns (e.g., desires that are usually self-centered such as desiring fame, status, greater beauty, or more sex) compassion, and wisdom.

Similarly, in Christianity or Aristotelian philosophy there are precise views of the ends to be achieved in a life that is lived well, and the process of getting to those ends is clearly articulated. Within Christianity, there is the belief in the Resurrection of Jesus, for example. There is the view that Jesus is a holy person, and to be Christian is to follow Jesus as someone to emulate. In Taoism, watchwords are simplicity, moderation, and humility. These are all views of "the good".

You can convert any section in this chapter and modify it completely so that it contains the precise steps on your spiritual path, if it is different from Tibetan Buddhism. Even if you don't consider yourself following a spiritual tradition, you may be strongly influenced by philosophy or psychology, and any section of this chapter could be rewritten or reconceived by you to embrace the ideas of that philosophy. For example, in Aristotle's philosophy there is a precise view of the good life, which is clearly discussed in his *Ethics*. In Adlerian psychology, a much more modern phenomenon, there is a view of "the good". For example, in Adler's worldview, importance is to be placed on education, the proper rearing of children and altruistic giving to others. Adler calls this altruism "social interest". Adler's "social interest" has been looked at previously and compared and contrasted to an enlightenment-oriented motivation. But these are all alike in that there is a view of "the good", although what exactly is "the good" in each case differs.

What is going to be presented in this chapter is, therefore, clearly aimed at embracing a certain set of ideas about the key ingredients of the good life. In other words, my view of "the good" is embraced by the Mahayana tradition, and freedom from suffering and movement toward greater compassion, creativity, real freedom, and supreme happiness is an important part of this view.

This is all in sharp contrast to most of the thinking in existentialism. In existentialism there is the belief that people create their own good, attach meaning to it, and then seek to actualize "the good" in their lives. Dyed-in-the-wool existentialists would point out that even in the Mahayana tradition or Christianity, you choose to adopt a view of "the good" for yourself – you are making a choice to adopt a certain phenomenology and a certain ideology, even if you are a scientist. Even existentialists make the existential choice of choosing existentialism! They choose to adopt the viewpoint that declares that there is not a specific view of "the good" – that it is for each person to construct. Sartre, Camus, Heidegger, Kierkegaard are philosophers whose writings embody this viewpoint. There is even a recently published political science textbook, *Modern Political Thought,* in which Raymond Plant argues that governments should be set up so that citizens can pursue their own view of "the good" in their own way, providing that they are not harming others by so doing.

To use a personal example, yesterday I was taking a walk on the shore of Lake Michigan with a friend. She described someone with whom she works. His view of "the good" is to have a large collection of rare books. He has an enormous collection and spends an incredible amount of time caring for the books. He even monitors the amount of humidity and sunlight within the large library in his home. In order to prevent the books from being damaged, he doesn't even allow himself or others to open them all the way, out of concern for cracking the binding or damaging the pages. While this sounds extreme and doesn't benefit anyone, from an existential standpoint it is fine. This man created meaning for himself and invests himself in this self-determined purpose.

The influential 20th-century psychologist, Albert Ellis, PhD, who has been cited earlier in this book and who is the main pioneer of cognitive behavioral therapy, strongly encouraged his clients to invent projects for themselves, which they considered to be personally meaningful. He said that it did not matter so much what the projects were, just that the projects were genuinely, creatively absorbing for the individual and not harmful to others – this is the existential viewpoint in practice.

The viewpoint advocated throughout this book, and perhaps particularly in this chapter, is clearly of the bent that there is a clear view of "the good" that I want you, the reader, to consider. However, from the viewpoint of a Buddhist practitioner, keep in mind that even views of "the good" are empty of inherent existence. They dependently arise and do not exist independently in and of themselves. Even the existential viewpoint is empty of inherent existence, as is Tibetan Buddhism, as well as any other Buddhism or spiritual path. This is a good thing, because it implies freedom, and infinite possibilities for you as you live and write Buddha Dharma or any other beneficial path in which you invest meaning.

The Peerless Path of Living and Writing Dharma

Some specific principles and activities that you can consider utilizing in order to guide your days of living and writing Dharma are as follows:

Remind Yourself of Freedom upon Awakening

You can begin each day by reminding yourself that you are free to pursue liberation and don't have to waste your time or life chasing after what people in Buddhist traditions call the eight worldly concerns. You could remind yourself of this freedom even before you open your eyes in the morning. You could remind yourself that the day before you is like a lifetime. You can use it to make progress toward freeing yourself from suffering and achieving the supreme happiness and real freedom which is enlightenment. You can use this time to make progress toward achieving realizations and overcoming obstacles.

Remember, when you have achieved ultimate wisdom and compassion, and overcome all obstacles, you will be entering the omniscient state of being a Buddha, which is pregnant with possibility to help others. You have just awakened from sleep, which is analogous to being born – and in fact, a new day has been born and is now before you. You can view each 24-hour cycle as being like a lifetime so as to make the best possible use of each day! The mind-body expert Ernest Rossi, PhD, has demonstrated that even *within* each day, every hour and a half our bodies go through an entire creative cycle which provides the opportunity for insight, creative problem solving, and the greatest awakening of our ability to better ourselves and others.

Remind Yourself of Taking Refuge

You can take refuge in what Buddhists call the three jewels, or remind yourself that you have taken refuge in them. The three jewels are the Buddha, his teachings, and the spiritual community of others who are practicing this tradition. If you are of another tradition, kindly remind yourself of what you sought protection and shelter in. Remind yourself to go forward into the day with a positive motivation to help yourself and others, and to cover some distance on your spiritual path in this day. What better day to make some good strides on your spiritual path than today? Remind yourself that today you have the shelter and the safety to make this progress.

Practice "Thought Training"

"Thought training" can be practiced throughout your day every day because through your thoughts you can change your suffering into happiness. Let's take an example. You have been doing two-hour writing sessions for two weeks in a row. Now today, due to job or family commitments, you simply don't have time for two minutes, let alone two hours of writing. You could see this as being extremely undesirable and make yourself very unhappy, but thought training gives you a very positive alternative.

A key to thought training is recognizing a situation or circumstance that initially appears undesirable, as actually being to your advantage and thus desirable in your writing or your life! Back to the fact that you don't even have two minutes to write today, whereas you have maintained two hours of writing per day for several weeks. Well, you can see this as desirable because you have a day off.

In writing, or any creating endeavor, removing yourself from the process for a while can have great benefits. Your brain literally gets an opportunity to make new neurological connections, which are going to take the form of new, inventive ideas, and writing that is very inspired. So after this day off, you can look forward to getting back to your writing on the following day with inspiration, originality, and productivity. This day off may even lead you to come back to your writing with some great idea that would have never dawned on you otherwise. Why not then celebrate this unexpected break and see it as desirable rather than rebelling against it and fretting about it?

At the end of this chapter, there is a worksheet about applying "thought training" every day on your day job. You can apply "thought training" in your work life, family life, writing life, or any part of your life to increase dramatically your freedom, flexibility, and potential for happiness! So, practice "thought training" in all kinds of situations throughout your day, every day, except don't be too hard on yourself if you decide even to take a day off from your "thought training" occasionally.

See Obstacles as Opportunities

On a much smaller scale, you can do this throughout your day – every day. For example, let us say that you are waiting to get a package from a literary agent in the mail. It does not arrive today, and you feel disappointed. You can tell yourself, "I am going to feel this disappointment *on behalf* of all beings." So, you will be turning an obstacle into an opportunity. In fact, you will also be practicing "thought training", because another "thought training" method not discussed above is experiencing a problem yourself as opposed to having others experience it. In other words, when you practice this technique, you have a problem and you tell yourself that you are going to have this problem so that someone else, or even everyone else, doesn't have to have it

Let us say you are having a difficulty with your meditation practice, doing a particular visualization and you experience a lot of internal distraction, and you feel frustrated. You can experience this frustration with the intention that all other people who are meditating don't have to have it. You will have changed an obstacle into an opportunity to help others. You will also have turned an obstacle in your meditation into something that is going to take you in the direction of ultimate freedom, compassion, and wisdom, which means enlightenment.

Project Positives

Another approach for the day, every day, is to project the positive onto yourself, other people and your entire environment. Essentially, this means pretending or imagining that you are enlightened, that everyone with whom you interact is enlightened, and that your environment is pure, spacious, and free, with limitless opportunities to be of benefit to others, and that you have the necessary capability and compassion. Is the benefit to increase your feeling of importance and self-preoccupation? No, in fact it's the exact opposite of this. By seeing yourself, imagining that you are already enlightened, then you can have an enlightened *motivation*, as well as thinking and acting with wisdom and compassion. You are going to become like that which, at first, you are only imagining.

In the recovery movement, there is a saying that goes like this, "Fake it till you make it." In other words, act in a socially responsible manner, with integrity, and in a loving way – and don't drink alcoholic beverages! – even if you don't really have these qualities yet. Similarly, by seeing others as being completely wise, completely free, and supremely compassionate, then you will treat them as enlightened. They will tend to project back this positive energy. Just as if you treat people in a hostile manner, they will tend to fight back. Well, instead of setting up retaliation, you are going to be setting up liberation!

In the Tibetan Buddhist tradition and other enlightenment-oriented traditions, those who are fully enlightened are in what is called a "pure land", unless they are living among us unenlightened people in order to help us. So, that is why you see your environment as being a "pure land". When you are attributing this to your environment, then you will treat that environment with honor, respect, and gratitude. As a result, it will actually become like the way you are viewing it and reacting to it.

Daily Practices or Prayers

In the Tibetan Buddhist tradition, practitioners who are at an advanced level take on the commitment to do certain meditation practices, every day, in order to achieve enlightenment as quickly as possible. It is usually recommended that the practices be done in the morning to ensure that they won't be missed, and because the mind is primed to respond to the practices as soon after waking up as possible. These meditation masters, even while sleeping, are doing something called the "Yoga of Sleeping" – meditation to help them build up positive karma and work toward becoming enlightened. When they wake up, this is the best time to do their daily practice commitments because their minds are most ready.

Whatever spiritual path you are on, I think that this practice is a good model. Even if your daily meditation or prayers are not something you have officially committed to do every day, why not do them in the morning when it is actually possible? What you do first thing in the morning is going to set the whole trajectory for your day.

Just as you can set the direction of your day in this way, you can also steer your consciousness in a positive direction while sleeping by praying, meditating, or reading beneficial material immediately before you go to sleep at night.

Optional Additional Practices

After your daily prayers or practices are completed, you can add others. For instance, in following the Tibetan Buddhist tradition, there are five meditation practices that I do every day. But once I finish these early in the day, I sometimes have time to do more yogas, which is another name for meditations. One of these optional practices is called White Tara, and it is a beautiful Tibetan Buddhist Meditation which is associated with longevity and healing. Kyabje Gehlek Rinpoche has a splendid book called *The Tara Book*, which was written with Brenda Rosen, and it is entirely devoted to the Tara practices. Another that I sometimes add after my commitments are finished, because it is a robust practice which leads to quick progress toward enlightenment, one called Ganden Lha Gyema. It comes from the 13th-century spiritual master Lama Tsongkhapa, who founded the Gelugpa tradition of Tibetan Buddhism, and of which his Holiness the Fourteenth Dhalai Lama is a descendent. With fondness for it, this tradition is often called the "Yellow Hat" school of Tibetan Buddhism in honor of the scholar's yellow hat that Lama Tsongkhapa wore and that are worn to this day by certain Tibetan Buddhist monastics.

Going into depth about the Ganden Lha Gyema practice goes well beyond the scope of this book, as does a discussion of Tara practices. So, a good source for you to consult if you're interested in learning more is *Ganden Lha Gyema: The Hundreds of Deities of the Land of Joy*, which is a transcript of instructions for the practice given by my teacher, Kyabje Gehlek Rinpoche. An excellent aspect of these practices is that although they are enormously beneficial, they do not involve an actual daily commitment. I apologize for only being able to whet your appetite for these practices, but by all means do delve into them on your own if the mention of their names sparks a bit of interest within you.

If yours is the Catholic tradition within Christianity, daily prayers for you may involve the Lord's Prayer, the Hail Mary, and the Prayer of Saint Francis. You are probably in the habit of starting your day with these practices. When you have the opportunity, go ahead and accelerate your spiritual development by adding additional prayer later in the day. For example, you could add the wonderful 12th-century *Lectio Divina*. This stands for meditation on scripture. A great little book that describes this practice as it relates to St Teresa of Avila is called, *Lectio Divina and the Practice of Teresian Prayer*. In short, Lectio Divina involves reading a segment of scripture, meditating on it, praying that you will be able to develop the virtues represented in the scripture, and putting these virtues into practice in your daily living.

Another excellent practice within the Catholic branch of the Christian tradition is centering prayer, which has its origins in the Christian mystics such as St John of the Cross. However, the leading contemporary exponent of it is the monk Thomas Keating, whose terrific book is called, *Open Mind, Open Heart*. Centering prayer mainly involves sitting quietly for about a 20-minute period, allowing yourself to experience the presence of God, and repeating a holy word or request to yourself, again and again, such as "Jesus, come."

If your tradition is the conservative branch within Judaism, in addition to saying the daily prayers and adhering to other daily practices, go ahead and increase the spiritual robustness of your life by delving into material such as Abraham Joshua Heschel's book *The Sabbath*, or Rabbi Laibl Wolf's book called, *Practical Kabbalah: A Guide to Jewish Wisdom for Everyday Life*. Or, what about

Walking the Bible, to use the title of an inspiring book about visiting the holy places connected to the very roots of Judaism, as well as its biblical heroes and heroines. Visit the holy places of your spiritual tradition and fully live the wonder that led to the archetypal images that have come to be known as your faith tradition to breathe their life into you.

The idea is this – don't simply do the minimum! Rather, in practicing Buddha Dharma or any sublime path, fully immerse your living and writing in its flavor.

Avoid Negative Consequences

Throughout your day, it is important to steadfastly work at reducing your negative emotions, thoughts, and behavior that would have negative consequences. From a Tibetan Buddhist standpoint, we would call these negative consequences "karmic", and they can be reduced through Mahayana methods such as "thought training", which has already been discussed above, and will be used by you extensively in *Assignment 10.2: Celebrating Failure and Rejection Practice* and *Assignment 10.3: Transforming Your Employment Into Your Path*. Cognitive behavioral therapy techniques, including the Five-Column Technique, acting against beliefs that are irrational and self-cherishing, and Rational Emotive Imagery, are effective in reducing negative consequences especially if practiced with supreme motivation.

A Mahayana Buddhist method of eliminating the negative emotions is wisdom. That is wisdom concerning the manner in which all things really exist – they are empty of true or permanent existence. They *do* exist in a conventional way, but they exist dependently and lack *inherent* existence.

You may be asking yourself, "How is this understanding going to help me eliminate my negative emotions?" The reason is that it is so freeing that you don't develop unhealthy attachments, addictions or hatred and anger toward people. You see their existence as boundless, free, and not restricted to your own ego's agenda! So, you are free of all the negative emotions, thoughts, and actions that would result if you had been lacking in this type of wisdom.

Let us say that you receive criticism from your boss or supervisor at the company at which you are employed. You may have the thought, "Maybe they are going to get rid of me, and eliminate my position because they are dissatisfied with me. Maybe they have already made up their minds about this." You might have felt anxious especially due to the latter part of this self-statement; *they have already made up their minds*. With Tibetan Buddhist wisdom you can completely cut through the suffering that has arisen from this unenlightened understanding. They may have made up their minds – the circumstance does exist *presently* – but you have an understanding of the *way* in which things exist. They arise interdependently and are impermanent. Therefore, you are free to exercise your abilities to change them! So, there *is* a chance of your keeping your job.

Yet even if you do lose the job, you can use "thought training" and recognize this undesirable circumstance as actually being good. It could be used by you as an opportunity to find a job to which you are a lot better suited, and perhaps you had even been thinking about doing that for a long time but wouldn't have acted, left only to your own devices. If it were not for emptiness, none of this would be possible.

It is this view of existence that makes it possible for you to attain complete liberation and for you to guide other living beings toward the state of perfect, complete enlightenment, regardless of how long it takes. Your current state of not having overcome all obstacles and not having achieved all realizations is empty of intrinsic existence, and it is impermanent. If you are reading these words, then you have obtained the precious human form with all of its endowments, and so forth, and you *can* achieve all realizations and overcome all obstacles. You *can* achieve enlightenment for the benefit of all sensitive beings, and to guide them to this state of unlimited compassion, skill and wisdom.

Most of this book is about positive things to do to increase the flavor and fire of your living and your writing. This section is about things *not* to do. Avoid doing things that will have negative consequences, for yourself or others. And whatever path you follow, this makes good sense, even if you do not necessarily have a religious orientation. In the Tibetan Buddhist tradition, negative karma can be purified, and in the Christian tradition, sin can be absolved, but go ahead and put real effort into staying away from what will lead to negative consequences in the first place. This will increase your freedom to pursue the positive directions identified in the other sections as well as your bliss, flow, and ability to benefit others.

Auspicious Role Models

It is important to focus on auspicious role models that will help you to advance your spiritual development, as you move toward becoming enlightened and are striving to live Buddha Dharma more fully. Sometimes being mindful of auspicious role models, and seeking to emulate their behavior, will help you make progress even more quickly than doing spiritual practices. Certainly, these role models would include people like His Holiness the Fourteenth Dalai Lama. You would be mindful of what he would do in a particular situation in which you find yourself, and then you can put the inspiration that comes to mind into practice. You can learn about him by reading his two-volume autobiography, as well as his authorized biographies.

Even as you read these books, especially if you are taking them to heart, this alone can help you make spiritual progress. You may be wondering how just this reading can help you to move forward in your spiritual development, but remember that we all have mirror neurons in our brains. These are neurons that specialize in causing us to experience vicariously whatever we are watching or reading – anything we are picturing in our minds. Within the Buddhist traditions, other auspicious role models might be Thich Nhat Hanh, Suzuki Roshi, Pema Chodron, Thubten Chodron, and Gehlek Rimpoche, Robert Thurman, and Sakyong Mipham, to name just a few individuals. Read about them, listen to them speaking, read their books including their biographies or autobiographies, and seek to emulate their virtues in your own life. This is a very rapid way to make spiritual development, especially if you are also implementing the other 10 principles in this chapter for fully living and writing Buddha Dharma.

What if you are of a different spiritual tradition – Judaism, for example? Elie Wiesel has always been a person whom I have admired as he lives and writes about his tradition in such an eloquent manner. Other figures include Abraham Joshua Heschel, Rabbi Akiba, Maimonides, Rabbi Hilell, and Martin Buber, to name just a few. For Christians, candidates would certainly be Jesus, his disciples, Origin, Saint Augustine, Saint John of the Cross, Saint Francis of Assissi, Thomas Merton, Albert Schweitzer, Mother Teresa, Martin Luther King Jr., and so many others! Within the humanist tradition, role models would be people like Socrates, Epictetus, Benjamin Franklin, Albert Einstein, Alfred Adler, and many others.

As a rule of thumb, think about the qualities that you want to emulate more fully in your life, and then study the authorized biographies of people within your tradition who embody those characteristics. Occasionally read material from a significant spiritual figure outside of your tradition. Then you can creatively apply their wisdom to how you live your life every day. Doing this, even by itself, will provide a tremendous boost to your spiritual development, and your ability to live and write Buddha Dharma or the aspects of your own path, if it is different.

Transforming Conventional Employment into Golden Elixir

You may have full-time or part-time employment that probably takes up a substantial number of your waking hours. Therefore, having the best enlightenment-oriented motivation during as much of your time of employment as possible is essential. With this motivation, and being mindful of having it, your work is spiritual practice, positive karma is generated, and you make progress on the path to total freedom and supreme wisdom, which means enlightenment.

Once again, with a buoyant enlightenment-oriented aspiration, your employment is not just what you do for a living – your altruistic drive transforms it into golden elixir. Your work becomes a key part of your path to enlightenment, and similarly, it becomes a key part of your path to salvation, to use the language of the Christian tradition.

In addition, others in the workplace will benefit tremendously from your bodhisattva activities there, in ordinary, everyday ways, and in their own spiritual development. *Assignment 10.1: Transforming Your Employment Into Your Path* is entirely devoted to helping you change as much of your time at work as possible into spiritual practice and enlightened service.

Dedication of Accumulated Merit

In the Buddhist tradition that I follow, which is the Mahayana path, there is a practice of dedicating the merit that you accumulate from engaging in positive, bodhisattva activity. This could include, for example, virtuous activity at work or from writing with the motivation to serve others or even meditating with the intention of having this better prepare you to help others. In saying "merit", I mean the positive karma that is accumulated from doing something out of an enlightenment-oriented motivation, to help others.

In the Mahayana tradition, we do something very remarkable with this positivity that we have accumulated. As soon as we recognize the accumulation we give it away mentally. In other words, say to yourself, and mean it from the bottom of your heart, "I give away this goodness that I have just accumulated for the benefit of everybody else." So, for example, every time you do a bodhisattva deed at work and record it on your *Buddha Dharma Performance Form (see Worksheet 10.1)* you can immediately dedicate it to everyone's spiritual evolution. The rationale for this is that people who are consciously not on an enlightenment-oriented path need this more than you do, so as someone who wants enlightenment for everyone, you'd better give it away to them! Finally, and maybe most dramatically, by giving it away – by this great generosity – you are building up even more good karma. When you dedicate, everyone wins!

Live Like Shakyamuni Buddha

By traveling along the peerless path of living and writing Buddha Dharma, you will be traveling in the direction of becoming like Shakyamuni Buddha, the historical Buddha who lived and achieved enlightenment some 2,500 years ago. You will do this by bringing to life, in your own life, the daily principles of living and writing Buddha Dharma every day from this chapter.

Of course, whatever tradition you are following, you can simply substitute the content of your faith tradition as the content for each of these principles and just use my structure. Then you can move in the direction of becoming like the heroes and heroines of your faith tradition, such as becoming more like Jesus, Mohammad, Maimonides, Lao Tzu, Krishna, Mother Teresa, or Socrates.

In any event, by living and writing in any of the enlightenment-oriented traditions, you are going to be producing massive amounts of new neurological connections in your brain every day.

The growth in your spiritual development will take place side by side with your brain development. New synapses will be formed, new connections made, new wiring activated to bring about that great wisdom, compassion, and abandonment of the things that used to seem important but now you know aren't really that important in life. As this happens, you will grow not only in the amount of intelligent faith but in the type of faith that you have.

In a wonderful book, *Stages of Faith*, the Harvard Divinity School professor James W Fowler shows that there are six stages of faith. Most people never get beyond the third stage, which he calls Conventional Faith. But the sixth stage, which is the highest, is called Universalizing Faith. He cites people like Buddha, Ghandi, Thomas Merton, Mother Teresa, and many others who embody Universalizing Faith. People at stage six are enlightened. They have shed the cloak of conventional worldly concerns, and act based upon internalized values, great wisdom, and profound compassion. Don't sell yourself short by stopping short of Universalizing Faith yourself!

Exercise your brain, spirit, and interactions with others every day to move toward joining the ranks of the great figures mentioned above. Don't just do this for your benefit, but go for it in the enlightened sense of doing it for the benefit of others. To help propel you in this direction, I have included assignments at the end of this chapter, and in these I hope that you thoroughly immerse yourself and accelerate your spiritual progress dramatically. This will prepare you for Chapter 12, which deals with contributing to changing the world.

Assignment 10.1:
Transforming Your Employment Into Your Path

As I have introduced earlier in the chapter, many of your waking hours are probably spent at your job, which involves some type of conventional employment. Now you have the opportunity to transform your job into part of your path to achieve enlightenment. This is going to involve being a bodhisattva in the workplace.

Being a bodhisattva in this setting involves having the enlightenment-oriented motivation to liberate yourself and others from suffering and to bring about great happiness for yourself and others. I am going to provide you with two forms that you can use throughout your workdays, and evenings, to transform your job into a major part of your path.

If your enlightenment-oriented motivation and actions only take place when you are on your meditation cushion, and if when you are at work you simply cannot wait to get out of there as quickly as possible, you are not going to help yourself or others very much in the journey to supreme happiness and wisdom. What you want is for your work to be a place for the performance of what you have been practicing in your Buddha Dharma practices or enlightenment-oriented practices from another tradition. Your aim is to see your work as an integral part of your spiritual development. Where better to perform your enlightenment actions and perspectives than in your workplace and family?

First, you are going to be provided with the *Worksheet 10.1:Buddha Dharma Performance Form*. As always, make plenty of copies of this form before writing on the original. On it, you are simply going to record everything that you do at work in a given day that has an enlightenment-oriented motivation behind it. You are going to write down everything that you do with the intention of benefiting others. For example, you might record something as simple as opening the door for someone, and you might even imagine as you are doing this that you are opening the door to liberation for this person, either now or in the future. If it's particularly difficult for you to open doors, then that makes this an even greater bodhisattva act. For example, I've broken both of my wrists several times. I still have some ongoing difficulty with them, and so it takes some real effort for me to open doors, yet I feel all the more privileged when I am able to do so for others.

If you make even a minor change to the operations that you supervise that slightly improves the safety for your workers, note this on your form. If you really pay attention to someone when they are speaking, especially if your natural impulse would be to disregard this person, write this on your form. On the worksheet, include mental activities that you do for the benefit of others. For example, there is a practice in which you breathe in all of the negativity and bad karma in a room in the form of dark smoke. Then, you visualize your heart as being like a pristine diamond and you see your body and the diamond purifying the dark smoke completely. When you exhale, you imagine that this is healing energy, ambrosia, which cleanses and brings happiness to all of the people in the room. If you perform this during a meeting at work, you would make note of it on *Worksheet 10.1.*

Then, in the column provided, write the "weight" of your bodhisattva action, as you subjectively see it, on a scale of 1 to 10, with "1" being the weakest and "10" being the strongest. For example, holding the door open for someone may be a "2", whereas being honest with someone in a situation where it would be more convenient to slant the truth might get a "6". You are writing different numbers because the karmic weight of the consequences of these actions differs. For example, were you to save someone's life at work, this would obviously get a "10+++"! Let me repeat that these ratings are subjective. You may see something that you do as having only a small weight, whereas in fact it may be highly beneficial to the person or persons to which it was directed, or vice versa.

The purpose of writing all this down should be virtuous, to

build your awareness of the good things that you are already doing, and provide yourself with a little bit of incentive and reinforcement to keep on doing more and more, and greater and greater bodhisattva deeds.

You will find that a by-product of regularly completing a *Buddha Dharma Performance Form* at work greatly infuses your work life with meaning. A job that you may have previously seen as futile and pointless may burst forth with value on the first day that you begin to record activities on the form. You will find yourself thinking creatively in every situation. How can I do even a tiny thing to make this work situation a bit better? Questions like these will become like watch words, and you will begin to live your work life around them, becoming much happier, productive, free, creative, and bursting forth with meaning and fulfillment as well as actual benefits to others. Ironically, some of you may find yourself, for the first time, actually living close to your job description, doing what's expected of you, having co-workers appreciate you more, and even getting good performance evaluations. In rare exceptions this won't be the case, but largely the job description for any individual involves benefiting those around them, and ultimately benefiting the company and the customer.

You will also find yourself being mindful of interdependence. This is a basic Buddha Dharma concept, but it is as true in organizational life as anywhere. You are going to become more aware of how you are dependent on co-workers, managers, customers, and so forth, and how all of these are dependent on you. As you become more and more positive, you will have a greater impact on everyone with whom you are interdependent at work. So, seen through this lens, can't there be a lot of meaning and fulfillment in almost any job, from CEO to street sweeper?

Next is *Worksheet 10.2: Situation or Circumstance Transformation Form*. On this form, you are simply to list the situations in a given day or during a given week, that you are able to transform through your mind. Lama Zopa Rinpoche said that, "Recognizing undesirable situations as desirable is the key to the thought training practice. It is the way to transform suffering into happiness."

Let me give an illustration of how I applied this wisdom in my job recently. Another manager wanted to change the composition of the therapy groups in the treatment center at which I am employed, and I objected because I saw this leading to countless extra hours of work. But I lost in the negotiation, despite my ardent protests. For a few hours, I went around seething with anger at the manager who had proposed what I saw as a preposterous recommendation, and then getting her way on top of that!

But there was little I could do because even after I talked to the CEO privately (he had been present at the meeting), he thought that there was a more compelling argument for changing the group composition. All I could change was my *mind*, or else go about seething with anger. But how could I see this situation as actually being desirable?

I almost immediately thought that, if nothing else, this change would lead me to sharpen my problem-solving skills concerning the extra work. Following this insight, I remembered that whenever you increase your problem-solving skills and learn anything new, brain growth increases alongside. As remarkable as it sounds, immediately my anger vanished and was replaced by enthusiasm about stimulating my brain. Indeed, I found that work became like solving a puzzle, and in a fairly short period of time I became more efficient, with none of the expected long hours slaving over my notes. Putting puzzles together has been described by Ernest Rossi, PhD, as one of the types of activities that rapidly stimulate the brain and produce new growth.

Every day, when I put the puzzle of the work notes together, I rejoiced and felt all the more happy. This manager, with whom I had been so angry, was actually helping to stimulate my brain

Worksheet 10.1: Buddha Dharma Performance Form

Date	Bodhisattva-Motivated Activity	Recipient(s) of Thought or Action	Karmic "Weight" (Scale 1–10)

Worksheet 10.2 Situation or Circumstance Transformation Form

Date	"Undesirable" Situation or Circumstance	How can I see this situation as desirable to transform my suffering into happiness?	Positive Qualities Brought to Awareness

growth on a daily basis – what an unexpected gift! Additionally, this thought transformation experience of mind greatly bolstered my confidence to effectively handle similar changes in the future in a constructive and even enthusiastic manner.

So, on your *Situation or Circumstance Transformation Form*, record all your successes on transforming unhappiness into happiness on the job! You can do this anytime you face a challenge at work or experience anything that you initially see as undesirable by asking yourself, "How can I see this situation as desirable?" This is, of course, assuming that you can't change the situation yourself in a positive manner, or can't do so right away. If you can change the situation, in a bodhisattva-like manner, then go ahead and do so, and if you cannot, then change your *mind* about the situation, and record the fact that you did this on the *Situation or Circumstance Transformation Form*.

Chapter Eleven

CONTRIBUTE TO THE TRANSFORMATION OF THE WORLD

First I'm going to review all the progress that you have made before I give you your final assignment, which is about transforming the world through changing global consciousness, and then I'm going to cut you loose to do just that.

The Progress You Have Made

You started off by identifying yourself as one of the target readers for this book, because of wanting to be a writer who basks in, and infuses others with, loving kindness and wisdom. Then, in Chapter One, you learned about the philosophical roots of this book, which are Western cognitive behavioral therapy and Eastern religion – Tibetan Buddhism in particular. You were assigned to marinate your mind, body, and spirit in inspired sacred texts to fully ripen yourself for enlightened writing and living.

Chapter Two showed you how to cut through the cognitive distortions and key root delusions that keep you glued to suffering, and away from boundless living, bliss, and liberation. In Chapter Three, you took this cutting process further by ridding yourself of ten irrational, self-preoccupied beliefs about writing and living – replacing them with enlightenment-oriented philosophies. You developed individualized enlightenment-oriented self-statements to further propel yourself along this path. In Chapter Four, you mastered two of the most skillful means for ridding yourself of distorted thoughts and root delusions.

Having the ability to rid yourself of distorted thoughts and root delusions, such as anger and ignorance, you developed the sublime capacity to be unconditionally serene or content and fully free from addiction – which is the sense that you *need* this or that in order to have serenity. Having unconditional serenity, you became free to fully liberate your creative energies in the present moment and develop a process-orientation, which is characterized by flow, optimal creativity, and an incredible ability to benefit other beings through your robustly enlightened living and writing.

This moved you to Chapter Seven, where you recognized fully the auspicious nature of your precious human life and you became determined to make the most of your life, initially through meditating upon and ultimately "seeing" the wisdoms of auspiciousness, mindfulness, and emptiness. This freed you to appreciate and tap into the eight forms of transcendent wisdom discussed in Chapter Eight. You began to record your insights upon awakening in the morning, and you acquired the knowledge of how to transform these morning notes into a completed manuscript through formulating and writing explicit questions, from which you crunched out the chapters of which your manuscript consisted. You are completing these chapters within writing sessions that last for up to two hours a day.

In Chapter Nine, you learned how to go from manuscript to market with a well-written book proposal. In that chapter, you also learned how to reinforce your own tenacity, because this quality is often needed to bring even the best manuscripts into bookstores, through publication. The next chapter showed how to go further by absorbing the Buddhist principles into your whole way of life and transforming your employment into the golden elixir of spiritual living. And now that you can do these things, you are ready to contribute to transforming the world at the highest level, which is an assignment that will last a lifetime.

Assignment 12.1:
Contribute to the Transformation of the World

Your last assignment is to make a contribution to transforming the world by changing global consciousness. If you were not already an enlightenment-oriented writer when you started this book, by now you have joined the movement! And the movement is to change the world through your enlightenment-oriented words.

You only need to stay in contact with the news for a single day to know that we are in very dire predicaments. There is terrorism, war, homicide, genocide, economic exploitation, unemployment, lack of medical care, starvation, epidemics, pandemics, dictatorships – this sentence could be ten pages long! But you have powerful spiritual technologies at your disposal that are capable of bringing about the solutions to these problems. What is more, you have the know-how to put these technologies on paper in book form and effectively communicate them to others.

Your published books may directly reach 1,000 people, 10,000 people, 100,000 people, a million people, or more. By reading your books, the consciousness of all these people can be changed in a positive direction. Then, your readers' new consciousness can impact on innumerable others, and lead them in a direction characterized by freedom from addiction, compassion, and wisdom. In this way the consciousness of the entire planet can be changed in a positive, fulfillment-oriented and enlightenment-oriented direction in which the fuel of the mind can be used to free people from suffering, as opposed to finding better ways to fuel vehicles of combat. The battlefield can shift toward the destruction of distorted thinking and anger, and the replacement of them with serenity and contentment. You can personally be an effective instrument of destruction of distortions, delusions, anger, and ignorance through your written words, the minds that they will influence.

One book can cause a paradigm shift of consciousness in the entire world. The world is filled with examples of this. If there had not been writers like the British philosopher John Locke, the marvelous democracies that exist in countries like the United States and the United Kingdom would not have been formulated. This philosopher, mainly through the book, *Two Treatises of Government*, formed the basis of the thinking of Thomas Jefferson, and other influential men who contributed to the development of the Constitution of the United States.

In other words, don't settle for a small impact. Settle only for a gigantic one. And of course, this impact starts by impacting your own living and writing, and doing so in small ways, day after day. But you can still have the inspiring goal of changing conditions throughout the world in a positive direction through the books that you write. Of course, you don't have to write books about government to do this. Instead, start with your own area of expertise, and work on influencing that domain. In your own way, and through your own field of expertise and the mastering of additional ones as necessary, bring about a new, new world! It may take a lifetime and it may take many lifetimes but don't shrink from the challenges because, equipped with your enlightenment-oriented science and ability to communicate this through the written word, you can meet it head on.

Now you are ready for your final meditation, which involves contributing to dramatically changing the world. Get ready to imagine dramatically changing the world, in practically every respect, in terms of it becoming an enlightenment-oriented planet, which embraces and cherishes all of the core truths of all the main world religions.

Get into meditation mode in your normal meditation space and breathe slowly in through your nose and out through your mouth.

> See the books of the past influencing the people of that time. For example, see the founding mothers and fathers of

the United States reading the works of John Locke, David Hume, and so forth. Or, visualize the men and women who contributed to the Constitutions of Great Britain, Canada, or Australia reading the material that truly motivated, enlightened, and inspired them to create the Constitutions that they brought into being. By doing this, you will be grounding your meditation in happenings which have already occurred.

Next, see yourself at the highest stage of spiritual evolution that you can imagine and visualize every aspect of yourself in marvelous detail. See yourself completing your first book, or your next book, whichever is the case.

In continuing your meditation, see yourself composing a very compelling book proposal, and sending it to just the right publishing companies or agents. Then see yourself signing the contract, going through the process of making revisions that will optimally benefit your readers, and see your book as it first appears on the market. Imagine, in your mind's eye, people reading your book and becoming inspired and enlightened, and then see these people inspire and enlighten multitudes more. Visualize the same thing multiplying further as your readers attend workshops, retreats, and are interviewed on television and radio. See world leaders reading your books – and the books that your readers may now be writing – so that they become more tolerant, patient, generous, contemplative as well as action-oriented and altruistic as a result. They thereby set up structures that benefit millions of people within their countries, such as hospitals, social welfare programs, educational institutions and so forth.

You can also visualize your heart as being like a pristine diamond that emanates tremendous amounts of light, which travel throughout the world and perhaps throughout the universe. By the purity and power of this light, military establishments are transformed into monasteries (of all the world's great faith traditions), nuclear weapons are turned into huge containers of food and medicine for the hungry and sick, and abusive and totalitarian regimes become democracies or empires governed by benevolent philosopher kings or bodhisattva saviors! See all of these transformations, and any more that you can visualize come into being simply by being touched by the light which emanates from your pristine, enlightened, diamond heart.

Parents who were abusing their children become transformed into parents who are nurturing their children in the most loving ways imaginable, prisons filled with inmates and electric chairs and gas chambers are transformed into aesthetically pleasing educational institutions that easily produce the wisest, most benevolent, and compassionate people that have ever existed.

You are assigned to do this meditation on a daily basis – and to take concrete action in this regard through your writing, workshops, audio products, interviews, articles, other vocational activities, parenting activities, and so forth – until your meditation becomes reality, regardless of how long it takes, even if it takes many lifetimes! Yes, even if it takes writing and living for your lives and the lives of all living beings, without any exceptions.

End Notes

Introduction

[1] Mahayana Buddhism is a type of Buddhism that is practiced in Tibet, parts of India, and other countries, and recently it has spread to the West. It is known as the Great Vehicle because the Mahayana Buddhist practitioners have, as their goal, not only their own enlightenment, but also the enlightenment of all other living beings, without any exceptions, regardless of how long this takes to accomplish. This is thought to be possible because, in this tradition, there is the belief in reincarnation and, therefore, your own reincarnations can continue to work toward this goal. His Holiness the Fourteenth Dalai Lama, Tenzin Gyatso, is surely the most popular member of this Buddhist tradition today. The Dalai Lama's line of incarnations extends back to the time of the historical Buddha 2,500 years ago, and back from there into mythical timelessness. In most other types of Buddhism –Theravada Buddhism, for instance – the practitioners mainly have as their goal only their own enlightenment. That is to say, overcoming their own suffering and attaining nirvana, which is a state of serenity or peace in which there isn't any more suffering.

[2] Enlightenment is a state in which a person has overcome all obstacles and attained all spiritual realizations in order to have supreme wisdom and compassion, and have the know-how to help other living beings overcome suffering and obtain their own enlightenment. They have the ability to use these skillful means fully. An enlightened being is a human being who has obtained enlightenment. In Tibetan Buddhist and most Buddhist belief systems, only human beings are able to obtain enlightenment. Living beings who are unenlightened, in the Tibetan Buddhist cosmology, are referred to as sentient beings,

and all living beings who are unenlightened – in addition to humans – fall into this category. Buddha nature is the potential within all human beings to obtain enlightenment.

[3] Karma is the result of your actions which can include what you say, do, and even what you think and feel. For example, hateful thoughts, the emotion of anger, and aggressive behavior all have negative karmic consequences. On the other hand, loving thoughts, feelings of empathy, and loving behavior have positive karmic consequences – they produce positive karma. Karma remains dormant until it ripens and sometimes this is immediately. Negative karma will ripen as something bad in your life, and positive karma will ripen as a positive happening in your life. Since, in the Tibetan cosmology, there is a continuity of consciousness through reincarnation, events taking place in your lifes now could be the result not only of karma accumulated in this life, but in past lives as well. You achieve enlightenment when you have accumulated a massive amount of positive karma and when all negative karma has been exhausted. So, you'll want to use up your negative karma, and build up your positive karma as quickly as possible. The ideas, techniques, and assignments in this book will help you in this pursuit—so do them whole-heartedly!

Chapter One

[4] Chapter 5 is devoted entirely to the topic of how you can overcome these and thereby achieve unconditional serenity. For simplicity, the eight worldly addictions have been distilled into the addiction to material acquisitions, sensual pleasures, approval, and happiness. If you believe that you MUST have any of these in order to have peace of mind (even happiness), then you are completely vulnerable to being taken out of your peace at any moment. In Chapter 5, you will learn how to reduce or rid yourself of this vulnerability entirely!

⁵ Bodhimind is the mind which seeks enlightenment in order to help all living beings become enlightened. So, this is the ultimate altruistic aspiration, which seeks to free all living beings from suffering and the causes of suffering, including the eight worldly addictions. When you have bodhimind then you are a bodhisattva. This is your first and most important step in freeing yourself and all other beings from the endless cycle of suffering, and delivering them to the sublime union of compassion and wisdom which is enlightenment.

Chapter Two

⁶ Sogyal Rinpoche is another of the great spiritual masters who was exiled from Tibet following the communist invasion of that country in the late 1950s. He has been incredibly influential in bringing Tibetan Buddhism to the West. He has teaching centers all over the world, and his most famous book is *The Tibetan Book of Living and Dying,* in which he summarizes, clarifies and expands upon the teachings in *The Tibetan Book of the Dead.* In these books, specific instructions are given for each stage of the dying process, so that one may obtain the most favorable rebirth that is possible, and therefore, be of the greatest benefit to other living beings. Teachings of this kind, although vastly important, are still very new to us in the West.

⁷ Samsara, as has been mentioned previously in the text, is the cycle of suffering into which we are reborn – rebirth after rebirth – until we obtain enlightenment. Nirvana is the intermediate state between samsara and enlightenment.

⁸ Shakyamuni Buddha is the historical Buddha who lived and achieved enlightenment some 2,500 years ago in India. When people think of the Buddha, this is who they usually have in mind.

Chapter Eight

[9] Tara is a female Buddha who is beautiful and radiant, and she is associated with healing in Tibetan Buddhist cosmology. Legend has it that she was formed from a teardrop of Avalokiteschvara, who is the illustrious Buddha of compassion. Aghast at the suffering of the world, Avalokiteschvara is believed to have cried, and one of his teardrops became Tara to heal people's suffering and afflictions. Tibetans have many practices based on Tara. The particular practice referred to involves White Tara, which is performed mainly for the purpose of physical healing.

[10] Taking refuge refers to seeking protection within the "three jewels" which are the Buddha, his teachings which are known as Dharma, and the spiritual community of Buddhist practitioners who are seeking enlightenment.

[11] Lam-rim is the name given to all of the basic teachings within the Tibetan Buddhist tradition. These teachings are also known as the graded path to enlightenment. In other words, as you master each level, you make progress toward enlightenment.

[12] Highest Yoga Tantra teachings and practices are known as the swift path to enlightenment. On this path, the goal of enlightenment becomes part of the path to getting there. You have to master the basic principles of lam-rim before you start taking initiations, and doing Highest Yoga Tantra practices. The words Highest Yoga Tantra and Vajrayana can be used interchangeably, and their meanings are identical.

[13] Literally, bardo means "the between". There are six bardos – the natural bardo of this life, the bardo of meditation, the bardo of sleep and dreams, the bardo of death, the bardo of dharmata and the bardo of becoming. As it is usually used by the people of Tibet, however, bardo refers to the experiences that occur

between one death and the next rebirth. And the bardo of becoming is the last phase before the next rebirth. Each of these bardos represents a distinct opportunity to obtain enlightenment for the benefit of all living beings.

[14] Lama Yeshe and Lama Zopa Rinpoche are two of the most influential teachers who have helped to preserve the Tibetan Mahayana Buddhist tradition. They founded the Federation for the Preservation of the Mahayana Buddhist Tradition (FPMT) which is headquartered in Portland, Oregon. They have thousands of students all over the world. Their book *Wisdom Energy* provides a concise, clear and inspiring description of the Mahayana Buddhist tradition.

[15] Chogyam Trungpa Rinpoche was the first great teacher to bring the Mahayana Buddhist tradition to the West. He was trained in "old Tibet" and escaped before the Chinese Communist invasion, which culminated in 1959. His teachings continue to be extremely influential.

Suggested Reading

Burns, David, 2006, *When Panic Attacks*, New York: Morgan Road Books

Cheever, Susan, 2004, *My Name is Bill*, New York: Washington Square Press

Ellis, Albert, 2005, *The Myth of Self-Esteem: How Rational Emotive Behavior Therapy Can Change Your Life Forever*, New York: Prometheus Books

Ignatius of Loyola, 2000, *The Spiritual Exercises of St. Ignatius*, New York: Random House Inc.

Maslow, Abraham, 1964, *Religions, Values and Peak Experiences*, New York: Viking

Otto, Rudolf, 1958, *The Idea of the Holy*, London: Oxford University Press

Rinpoche, Sogyal, 1994, *The Tibetan Book of Living and Dying*, New York: HarperOne

Thurman, Robert, 1998, *Inner Revolution: Life, Liberty, and the Pursuit of Real Happiness*, New York: Riverhead Books

Thurman, Robert, 2004, *Infinite Life: Awakening to Bliss Within*, New York: Riverhead Books

Thurman, Robert, 2005, *The Jewel Tree of Tibet: The Enlightenment Engine of Tibetan Buddhism*, New York: Free Press